Bridget's Hanging

Bridget's Hanging

Sheila Duane

For Dean, Jude and Bridget

Copyright © 2016 Sheila Duane
All rights reserved.

ISBN: 153334986X
ISBN 13: 9781533349866
Library of Congress Control Number: 2016908384
CreateSpace Independent Publishing Platform
North Charleston, South Carolina

Introduction

Bridget Deignan (a.k.a. Durgan, Dergan)[1] was hanged in New Brunswick, New Jersey, in 1867. Bridget was a twenty-two-year-old illiterate, poor immigrant from Ireland who was essentially exported from Ireland by British Protestant landowners who saw the poor and uneducated as an economic burden. She was shipped to Liverpool in 1866, then boarded a bark (a sailing vessel) called the *Orient*, which arrived in New York harbor only a few months before she was hanged for a crime she did not commit by citizens who despised Catholics and feared and distrusted immigrants.

I fell upon the story of Bridget's short, tragic life while reading a book called *Women Who Kill* by Ann Jones. Jones wrote about Bridget Deignan, accepting that she was probably guilty, but also convinced she'd been railroaded by a judicial system driven by a sense of superiority, a hatred of "Romanism" (Catholicism), and unrelenting greed.

Facts also indicate that the judiciary in 1867 New Brunswick was discriminatory, unsympathetic, and incompetent. Greed was a major factor in the way the trial and the defense were conducted, and the media's reporting on the case.

---

1 Bridget's last name appears in more than one spelling in published reports about her. For consistency, I have spelled her name "Deignan" throughout. However, I have retained other spellings when used in quoted materials.

Multiple individuals who lived in and around New Brunswick offered published copies of Bridget's "confession" prior to her execution. According to the *New York Times*, the recorder of the city, Mr. David T. Jeffries, "proposed to sell some time ago the confession of Bridget Durgan, and his modest price was $1,000 in gold. Another man named Randolph, who, we believe, is a gaoler under Sheriff Clarkson, had a confession, and we understand his price was $250 gold or currency, we don't know which. One of the evening papers is reported to have paid $50 for another confession not worth the paper it's written on" (31 August 1867). Bridget's own defense attorney, Mr. Garnett Adrian, also offered for sale a copy of his version of Bridget's confession, although Mr. Adrian at least had the decency to wait until after Bridget was hanged to do so. The *New York Times* correspondent was quick to point out that all of these confessions are wildly different. Further, several other confessions published as murder pamphlets, a popular read at the time, were published after Bridget's execution, including one by a "Rev. Mr. Brendan" (Rev. in this case being a self-imposed term of honor, not religious leadership). Research indicates he either never met her or may have briefly spoken with her once. Barclay & Company of Philadelphia published at least one other murder pamphlet, but it was printed without an author's name.

Regardless, Bridget was not a killer.

The following facts have been proven beyond doubt through vetted documentation:

Bridget was born in 1844 in Sligo, Ireland.
 She and her family lived in a Carrick-on-Shannon workhouse after losing access to British-owned property they'd farmed for more than ten years in Ireland.
 Bridget's father ushered her to America after the deaths of her mother, brothers, and sisters in the workhouse.
 She left Ireland by ship in 1866 and landed at Liverpool, England.
 Bridget left Liverpool in May 1866 aboard a bark called the *Orient*.

Bridget's Hanging

The *Orient* (and Bridget) landed in New York Harbor in June 1866.

She transitioned into American life at the Castle Garden Immigrant Center in New York City.

She left Castle Garden for the first time when she was hired by Lewis and Mary Dayton of Piscataway, New Jersey. She worked for them as a domestic.

Dr. William Coriell treated Bridget for "falling disease," or epilepsy, while she was working for the Dayton family.

She began working for the Coriell family as a domestic on October 22, 1866.

Mrs. Coriell was murdered on February 25, 1867.

These facts are not in question. The issue of Bridget's guilt, however, is in question. There is certainly evidence indicating she had foreknowledge that the Coriell home would be robbed on the evening of February 25, 1867. She was frightened and manipulated into remaining silent. And after the murder of Mrs. Coriell, Bridget was still, even while in jail, intimidated into silence. In this way, Bridget was guilty, but not guilty of murder.

The following is a story of fact and intuition. The factual story of Bridget's hanging is documented. Her personal narrative, based on research and the exchange of ideas about social histories, the sensibility of Irish poverty, and the myths that sometimes sustained immigrants fleeing destitution, is intuition.[2]

The newspaper articles that have been included here are not photocopies, as permission for reprinting was not granted. Because the newspaper content is no longer under copyright, the exact text of the articles has been reprinted (with original spellings and punctuation marks as printed) without the images from the newspapers referenced. Throughout this text, the *New York Times* will be abbreviated *NYT* in citations.

---

2 According to archivists at the New Jersey State Archives, the Middlesex County Court of Oyer and Terminer records once kept at the Middlesex County clerk's office, the depository for Middlesex murder trial records, may no longer exist. As documented by archivists, the Middlesex County clerk's office disposed of many "early" court records years ago. For this reason, most of the research provided here is from newspaper publications, census records, and published research materials.

One

From the *Marysville Daily Appeal*, Number 83, 6 October 1867:

The Hanging of a Woman.
The Daily Appeal.

Here is a representative illustration of the civilization of the nineteenth century: I am going to describe it with the utmost minuteness, so that, if possible, not a single incident, even the smallest, may escape the cognizance of every reader who is particularly fond of horrors. The hours between which it was declared by Peter Vredenberg, judge, that Bridget Durgan should be hung by the neck until dead, were ten A. M. and 2 P. M. on this delightful day of our Lord. Sheriff J. Manning Clarkson, who had the hanging to do, arranged to get through with it as early as possible in the cool time of the forenoon. Tickets had been issued for the occasion to perhaps five hundred people. A great many more than five hundred people were so anxious to be included in the list of witnesses that some of them suggested excellent bargains to the fortunate holders of tickets, which bargains were in every instance refused. A great sensation was anticipated, and talked about in a lively, and in fact, shocking, way. The walls of New Brunswick houses and hotels have rarely heard such interesting conversations on death as they heard last night.

Early this morning the jail vicinage was populous with hundreds of women, children, policemen, and soldiers in their shirt sleeves, each of whom was a commander. Order (such order!) was preserved, that there was a reasonable distrust lest a riot from some unseen quarter should break out at any moment. The five hundred people with invitation to attend the execution besieged the jail so early that every one of them was obliged to cool his heels at the jail door for an hour and a half before arrangements for admission were completed.

The doomed wretch within had been awake since five o'clock, at which time Father Rodgers, her confessor, called and administered to her the sacrament.

Her counsel, Mr. Adrian, called soon afterwards, but had only a brief farewell from her.

She ate a light breakfast of berries, milk and rolls. Again Father Rodgers, together with Fathers Dugan and Midziolis, called and talked of religion. Then two ladies, Mrs. Randolph, wife of the jailor, and Miss Sullivan came to say good-by.

Bridget's Hanging

The woman then addressed herself to her toilet, and attired herself carefully and well. She donned a brown merino or alpaca dress, a fresh white collar, a pair of high white linen cuffs, and a pair of white cotton gloves. Around her neck, besides, she put a black silk cord. Her hair was arranged with scrupulous care. The lover, for whom she might have dressed long ago in this fashion, was outrivaled now.

At half past nine o'clock, a few of those invited were admitted within the walls. Twenty minutes later the jail door was thrown open, and all who had tickets came pouring in.

It was disgraceful enough, shame enough, that this crowd should have been let in at all to witness such a scene, which I understand the law of New Jersey requires shall be private. But the behavior of the crowd was such as to disgust, but instruct, even an embryo philosopher. All sorts of people, all kinds of faces, old and young were present. The roofs of the sheds surrounding the jail were littered with agile climbers. So was every elevated position. All gazing weirdly at the gallows. The latter, which was nothing but two upright beams, and a cross beam, painted a dull lead color, and a rope run on pulleys aloft and dangling in the center nearly to the ground, had a different fascination to each spectator according to his caliber.

To some it was attractive as a piece of mechanism; it was thus viewed by the majority of critical eyes. Other eyes saw a phantom dangling beneath it, and grew bright. Other eyes shrunk away from it.

A body of inefficient deputies were at hand. A rope was stretched across an angle of the yard in front of the scaffold. A slight enclosure of boards inside of the rope had been erected for reporters of the press. A line, formed of constables and their batons horizontally extended, was formed between the scaffold and the door in rear of the jail, whence the condemned woman was to emerge. Among other jokes, freely and loudly uttered about this time, was one by a boy of eighteen:

"Hope to gad she hain't got no hoops. She'll have hard enough work getting through if she has."

A loud laugh.

Sheriff Clarkson busied himself with the adjustment of the rope.

"Fix it right, old man. Don't let her bump her head agin that beam," shouted a fellow in a red shirt, to the intense merriment of at least a hundred hearers.

"Git off that shed! pitch them fellows off. Sheriff, ha ha! nobody allowed on the shed!"

Really, this was very like a scene at a fair.

The Sheriff went into the jail, entered Bridget's cell, and placed the noose around her neck, she assisting, it is related, as the cord caught in her hair. A strap was then tied around her arms, pinioning them behind, just above the elbows. The death warrant was read outside the cell. Bridget listened to it, seated in a chair, without a word, but keeping up the odd twitching of her hands.

Fathers Rogers and Dugan were at her side. The rear door of the jail was thrown open. The prisoner, the two priests, and the Sheriff, emerged. The priests were clad in their appropriate robes, and supported the prisoner, one on each side, as she walked to the scaffold. What a delicious walk it would have been out in the fields, with no scaffold to go to, and no noose (a brutal contrivance, fit for the devil to have devised) about the neck. The sky was so clear: the breeze was so fresh and pure; the leaves of the trees waved so gently overhead!

But it is impossible to give this creature's memory any real solemnity whatever. Her march to the scaffold, her death, was in itself and by reason of its surroundings like the last walk and the death of an ox.

A shout was set up the moment the little procession appeared.

"Down with umbrellas!" "Hats off" "Stand back!" "Do get down!"

"D**nit, can't you let somebody see besides you?"

And a surge forward, right up to the front of the wretched woman about to be launched into eternal darkness, ensued. The reporters for the press, who were nearest, were crowded forward by the push. There was not an instant's silence or order.

The priests and the condemned were the only ones perfectly calm for a few moments. The former held the crucifix before their charge, who gazed upon it, not with a rapt, but still with an unwavering expression, of which her habitual approach to a smile was part.

The Sheriff, with fingers that looked pale, adjusted the noose to the cord above, saying, in a low tone, something to the poor wretch as he did it. She turned to him and spoke:

"I don't want any prayers for me in any Protestant churches."

Or:

"I don't want to be buried in a Protestant graveyard."

Something to that effect. Accounts differ, and the Sheriff is reticent.

The jailor pressed forward from behind. To him she gave a kiss, and said:

"You are not hanging an innocent woman."

That was all. An instant afterwards Sheriff Clarkson entered, alone, the little closed box alongside. The dull blow of an axe was heard.

All this, the murder that led to it (if Bridget Durgan's word to one of the witnesses at the trial can be taken) might have been prevented if Asa Bush had written those few lines.

J. B. S.

Bridget's Hanging

On August 30, 1867, twenty-two-year-old Bridget Deignan was hanged for the crime of murder in New Brunswick, New Jersey. At that time, most people in New Jersey and the surrounding states believed that Bridget was a brute, little more than an animal, who had willfully and violently murdered her employer for financial and personal gain. People believed this because that's what the newspapers printed—newspapers that sold more copies when the printed stories were more salacious, more agitating, more extraordinary. And Bridget's particular saga had all the makings of good crime drama: a lovely, sympathetic victim, Mrs. Mary Ellen Coriell, a genteel doctor's wife and the mother of a beautiful, healthy daughter named Mamey; a wicked, ignorant, immigrant housemaid and former prostitute who from jealousy and evil intent committed premeditated murder for bloodlust and self-gratification; and an arson fire that scorched the baby-fine hair of the murdered woman's daughter, set by the villain to destroy murderous evidence—a good story to be sure.

But there is another version of this tragedy in the subtext of the many newspaper articles and the multiple confessions that were marketed within hours of Bridget's death on the gallows. Was Bridget Deignan a murderer or a victim of economic and cultural prejudice? Any close reading of the documents and newspaper articles related to Bridget's case demonstrates that conclusive evidence was lacking, testimony was confused at best, perjury is certain in more than one case, and the motives of so many individuals involved were dubious or worse. Further, the men who crafted the confessions published after Bridget's death—who sold these confessions as books or pamphlets for what was a considerable amount of money in 1867—presented manuscripts in which Bridget admitted killing Mrs. Coriell in hopes of marrying Dr. Coriell, a fact that all the legitimate sources involved in the case dispute. Further, these false confessions contain factual errors that prove their speciousness, the first of which is Bridget's own name: Durgan. Her name was in fact Bridget Deignan; she insisted this to the *New York Times* reporter who spoke with her after her conviction.

It was, she stressed, her north Irish brogue that confused her identity to the residents of New Jersey and the reporters from New York and Philadelphia. The "confessions" also describe Bridget as a young woman who grew up in a relatively well-to-do family in Ireland, who left there after her father ended her relationship with a young man below her station. These alleged confessions describe her as a former prostitute and grifter whose purpose was to obtain money and status by any means possible, even murder. Research has proven that this is not the case.

Although Bridget was born in Sligo, Ireland, in 1844, as was written in newspaper articles and in the sham confessions, she was not born to a well-to-do family. In fact, she'd spent much of her life living in an Irish workhouse called Carrick-on-Shannon. This is one of the reasons, during the days following her arrest after the murder of Mary Ellen Coriell, she chose to keep silent about the identities of the actual murderers…her life in a jail cell in New Brunswick, New Jersey, was more pleasant than it had ever been outside of that cell. She'd spent the earliest years of her life in dire poverty, living near starvation on farmland infected by the potato blight fungus. By the age of ten, she was helping her father unload barges along the Killala Bay, living as a gypsy, eating cabbage and sleeping in barns or warehouses. Finally, after her father's lungs began to fail, the family sought refuge at Union Poor Law workhouses in Sligo and Boyle. Ultimately, they were admitted to the workhouse at Carrack-on-Shannon where she watched her family waste away from lung, bone, and joint tuberculosis. For Bridget, the prospect of revealing the truth about the night of Mrs. Coriell's murder, of verifying her own innocence, and achieving her release was less attractive than the expectation of spending the rest of her life in a warm, comfortable "gaol."

```
        Murder in NewMarket N.J.
        The Inquest Held Yesterday.
   Late on Monday night the people of New Market,
   Middlesex County, N.J. were startled by the
```

report that Mrs. Mary Ellen Coriell, the wife of Dr. William W. Coriell, a physician practicing in the village, had been murdered during his temporary absence from the house. Notice of the murder was given by the servant girl, who rushed from the house with the child of Mrs. Coriell in her arms, passed her nearest neighbors, and aroused a family living at a greater distance. On entering the house of Dr. Coriell, who had not yet returned, his neighbors found his wife on the floor of her sleeping apartment, clotted with blood, and already dead. No less than 25 wounds had been inflicted upon her face and neck, one severing the jugular vein. Of the wounds one was apparently from the impression of teeth, and others were stab-wounds inflicted by some sharp instrument. Her clothing and the walls of her apartment were stained with blood; feathers from her bed were thickly strewn over the floor, and the bed was on fire. The story told by a servant (an Irish woman, named Bridget Durgan, aged about 25 years) who had been living with the family for four months, was that early in the evening two men had called at the house and inquired for the Doctor. On being told by Mrs. Coriell where he had gone, they said they would go after him. About eleven o'clock a knock was heard at a door opening into the kitchen part of the house, and Mrs. Coriell told Bridget, who had the babe in her arms, to open the door for the Doctor. Almost simultaneously a knock was heard at the door opening into the hall, and Mrs. Coriell hastened to open this door herself. Two men immediately entered and Mrs. Coriell cried to Bridget, as if choking, "Go for the Doctor." The girl had hastened out of the yard, and when at the gate heard her mistress say, "Come back and help me. If you we're being killed I would help you." She did not return, however, but first went to the village store where some relatives of Dr. Coriell resided, and not succeeding in arousing them, came back to another house and there succeeded in arousing the inmates. She states that two weeks ago on Sunday she had a conversation with Barney Doyle and John Hunt, employees on the New-York Central Railroad at New-Market, when one of them said he "would have revenge of the Doctor dead or alive because he had killed Ellen Doyle's child." These men are thought in the neighborhood to be above suspicion, and though not directly accused by the woman as the perpetrators of the crime, she appears by innuendo to put the imputation upon them that possibly they are the men who entered the house and murdered Mrs. Coriell.

New York Tribune 27 February 1867

The trial of Bridget Deignan (Durgan) began on Monday, May 20, 1867. Bridget had been charged with the murder of Mrs. Mary Ellen Coriell, her mistress and employer. The murder had occurred in the early morning hours of February 25, 1867, and it had been accompanied by an arson fire that failed to destroy the Coriell home. Mrs. Coriell had been beaten and stabbed to death with a knife, it was alleged, from the kitchen of her own home. In the very early hours of that February morning, Bridget, holding Mrs. Coriell's infant daughter, Mamey, appeared at a neighbor's house. She'd trudged through mud, snow, and darkness with the baby to report that there were burglars in the Coriell home. She reported that Dr. Coriell was away, assisting in the delivery of a baby, and two men had come to the house looking for him. She said the men left but returned later to rob the house…the two men, she insisted, might be killing Mrs. Coriell…the house might be on fire. When Bridget appeared at the neighbor's home, she was wearing a white cotton slip with a large circular spot of blood on it. The child's hair was singed on one side, indicating that she'd been in the vicinity of the fire that was, possibly, at that moment burning in the bedroom of the Coriell home.

After being awakened and troubled by Bridget's insistence that her mistress needed help in her home, men in the neighborhood gathered to assess the burglary situation there, many believing that Bridget was overreacting, as she tended to be overly nervous at times. Instead, the neighbors found a fire burning in Mrs. Coriell's bedroom where her body was discovered, covered in blood and feathers from the slashed pillows and mattress in the room. She was dead, and her body revealed that she'd endured an extended assault.

For the next hours and days, Bridget's story regarding that evening repeatedly changed. At one telling, she did not know the identity of the men who called at the Coriell home; at another, she revealed that the two men were local men, Barney Doyle and Michael Hunt. Later, Bridget told the police a woman was with Doyle and Hunt on the night of the murder. She also indicated at one point that she'd been sworn to secrecy with respect to the intentions and identities of the killers. "If I do know who those men are, and if I tell, what will they do to me?" she asked, weeping (*Baltimore Sun* 28 February 1867).

The one consistency in her revelations was her own innocence of the murder. This held true even as local newspapers were printing her multiple "confessions." This article appeared two days after the murder in multiple newspapers.

Bloody Murder in New Jersey

```
A Servant Girl Kills Her Mistress with a Butcher
Knife
    New Market, Middlesex Co., N.J. Feb.26.The
wife of Dr. L. W. Coriell, in the absence of
her husband, was brutally murdered by the ser-
vant girl, on last evening, Feb, 25. It seems
that the girl and the wife of the Doctor had
some dispute, and she was discharged and was
to leave on the 27th. The murder was committed
with a butcher knife, and it seems that they
had a great struggle. Mrs. Coriell was cut in
twenty different places, one of the cuts sev-
ered the jugular vein.
    Upon examination, the girl made a full
confession.
```

National Republican 27 February 1867

When Bridget was arrested, Samuel Randolph, the jailer, asked his wife to bring Bridget some clean clothing that she could wear to sleep and to spend her days in some comfort. Samuel was concerned about imprisoning a female as ill as he'd been told Bridget was—an epileptic who would have seizures and sometimes lose consciousness for hours. She often seemed confused, and she was known to have problems related to her menses. Mary Randolph was more than happy to oblige, pleased to perform her Christian duty. And, as time passed, Bridget seemed to like living in the jail in New Brunswick. She'd never been happier. The jailer's wife, Mary, had become like a mother to her even though she was only twelve years older than Bridget. Caring, spiritual women developed an interest in her—in saving her soul. A local schoolteacher, Margaret Sullivan, had taken it upon herself to teach Bridget to read.

Bridget was allowed to bathe while in the jailhouse, sometimes three or four times a week. She'd never been allowed that in her lifetime: to idle in a large, tin plunge bath and soak in hot water. It was important that Bridget wasn't alone in the bath because a seizure could've caused her to drown and die without an audience.

Margaret Sullivan and Mary Randolph were friends. They attended the same church, the same prayer meetings, and were both dedicated to bringing a religious revival to New Brunswick. They were similar in many ways…both might have been called reformers except that Mary Randolph always insisted that reformers were women of means who marched and waved flags purchased for them by their wealthy husbands. Neither woman had a wealthy husband. Both women worked. Margaret was an unmarried schoolteacher, and Mary earned extra money doing laundry, working from her own home. Mary had no children of her own, but she offered herself as a foster mother to children in the area who had no parents or whose parents were ill or unable to take care of them. While Bridget was in jail, Mary had been caring for a young girl, an eight-year-old named Maggie, whose mother had one day simply disappeared. Mary constantly reassured Maggie that her mother would return, although no one was quite sure that was the case. When Mary went to the jail to visit Bridget Deignan and to read to her from the King James Bible or from books about the saints, she would often bring Maggie who was also learning to read and whom she was trying to teach about the dignity of human life.

Sheila Duane

Federal Census: see lines 7, 8, and 9
https://familysearch.org
(Specific URLs subject to change)

Bridget's Hanging

The first time Mary met Bridget in the Middlesex County Jail in New Brunswick, she immediately knew how ill Bridget really was. Her skin was pale—not beige or white, but a chalky yellow—and she was clammy, sweaty, and cool at the same time. Her eyes were half-open as though she was sleep deprived or intoxicated, and she appeared swollen rather than overweight. Sometimes she spoke lucidly; at other times, her logic seemed confused and her ideas discursive. Bridget was clearly nervous and was reluctant to make eye contact with Mary or anyone else. She seemed, however, quite pleased with the items of clothing Mary brought from her home for Bridget: warm, heavy cotton nightdresses that smelled of castile soap, underclothes, two belted cotton tunic dresses, one pink and one pale green, wool stockings, and slippers.

As Mary folded Bridget's soiled clothes to take home and wash, she noticed the ring of mud stain around the bottom of the skirt. For a moment, she thought about Bridget hurrying after midnight through the muddy snow carrying Mamey Coriell, looking for help in the dark for herself, for the child, and for her murdered employer. Mary could not imagine this woman in front of her, this frightened, introverted, and clearly infirm woman, participating in an extended beating and then stabbing murder of another woman, regardless of that woman's slight figure.

The New Jersey Murder.

```
An inquest was held yesterday on the body of Mrs.
Coriell, who was killed at New Market, N.J., on
Monday night, as reported in yesterday's EVENING
POST. On examining the body it was found that
twenty-three stabs had been inflicted by means of
a sharp table-knife which was used by the family.
The print of four teeth was also found on the
neck of Mrs. Coriell. On examining the teeth of
Bridget Durgan, the servant girl, they were found
to correspond exactly with the prints on the neck
of the murdered woman. The jury found a verdict
```

against the girl, and she has been committed to the Middlesex County jail to await her trial.
New York Evening Post 27 February 1867

Further, how could this woman, after an extended physical struggle, then carry a toddler through the muck of New Market's slushy, mud streets to call for help? This made no sense to Mary, so she asked Bridget directly if she'd killed her mistress. She assured Bridget she would not judge her, that she was there as a companion rather than a jailer and would keep the secret always…But she stressed she had to know the truth. Bridget assured her that she did not kill Mrs. Coriell, and that if she died at that moment, she would go to heaven. She insisted that Saint Peter would welcome her when she got to his doorstep. Mary Randolph would hear these words repeatedly for the next few months as she helped care for Bridget, as she watched Bridget through her fits of epilepsy, and as she bathed her and washed her hair. Bridget was adamant; she was not a killer.

Margaret Sullivan had asked her the same question. She stressed, too, that she wanted only to help her, to save her soul…And Bridget would insist, "I never killed nobody. Nobody's death is on my hands" (multiple sources). Margaret also believed her and grew to care quite a bit for Bridget. Margaret Sullivan and Mary Randolph became like family; they offered her friendship and promised her their advocacy.

Throughout the national and international newspaper coverage of Mrs. Coriell's murder and Bridget's trial, reporters and witnesses implied and, in some cases, asserted that is was difficult if not impossible to understand Bridget's northwestern Irish accent, often called a Hibernian brogue (sometimes called a Hiberno-English accent). This became clear as early as the second day of testimony in Bridget's trial when a neighbor, Reverend Little, testified that he had difficulty understanding anything Bridget said. His wife repeated the statement in her testimony, as did Cyrus Lowe and Harriet Hillyer, other neighbors. Such statements continued throughout the trial.

Bridget's Hanging

Linguistic scholars have studied not only grammatical differences between modern English and Anglo-Irish, but have described the English-Gaelic derivative languages of Ireland, especially prevalent during the nineteenth century, as close to Middle-English, especially among the poorest rural inhabitants of northern and western Ireland (Hickey). The fact that the people of New Jersey as well as reporters from every corner of the United States had difficulty understanding Bridget's accent clearly contributed to the differing newspaper reports of her statements, contrary testimony about her answers to questions asked in a single interrogation, and her own inability to make herself understood. She was foreign, of an alien religion, and difficult if not impossible to understand. Bridget's poverty and ignorance were manifest in her language.

As noted earlier, Bridget had never bathed in a plunge bath before. The jail had a tin plunge tub that stood against the stone walls in a small room on the south side of the jailhouse. In the room was a hearth across from a pot-bellied stove; on the round surface of the stove was a large pot filled with water that was always steaming. The room was kept incredibly warm, even in the winter of early March, and there was usually a teakettle there filled with water, never quite ready to whistle. There were wood stools standing near the hearth, and Mary would use a small-handled copper pot to fill the plunge tub with the hot water from the tin buckets that stood against the hearth. Because Samuel Randolph was devoted to his wife's compassion, he would bring more buckets of cold water and place them outside the small room to maintain Bridget's modesty. Mary would then bring in the buckets and pour the water into one of the two large pots against the hearth fire.

The first time Mary helped prepare Bridget for a bath, she suggested she should wash Bridget's hair. Bridget always kept her head covered—sometimes with a cotton scarf, other times with a small bonnet. And even before her bath, she didn't want to remove her head covering to have her hair washed. Mary suggested it would be a good idea so that perhaps, if there were lice in her hair, they could get them out to keep her cell mattress clear of bugs. Before she removed her scarf though, Mary had to promise Bridget she would not laugh. When she finally took it off, she revealed small bald patches on her scalp the size of pennies. As Mary washed her hair, Bridget explained how she had come to lose patches of hair.

Bridget told Mary that although she'd been born in Sligo, she'd spent most of her childhood in a workhouse in Carrick-on-Shannon, not far from Sligo. There had been an epidemic of tuberculosis in the workhouse, and it seemed everyone had become infected. The sick rooms or infirmaries, stone cells with low ceilings at the end of each dormitory block, were filled with older women and young children who coughed and bled from their mouths, with sweating, chalky-white skin, their eyes often bloodshot and teary. She said the illness had also spread to her family, but she was the lucky one.

The following are the records of the Deignan family deaths at the workhouse in Carrick-on-Shannon:

Bridget's Mother:
Bridget Deignan
Estimated Birth Year:	abt 1821
Date of Registration:	1865
Death Age:	44
Registration District:	Carrick-on-Shannon
Death Country:	Ireland
Volume:	18
Page:	40
FHL Film Number:	101582

Sister:
Ellen Deignan
Estimated Birth Year:	abt 1843
Date of Registration:	1865

Bridget's Hanging

Death Age: 22
Registration District: Carrick-on-Shannon
Death Country: Ireland
Volume: 13
Page: 40
FHL Film Number: 101582

Brother:
Luke Deignan
Estimated Birth Year: abt 1849
Date of Registration: 1865
Death Age: 16
Registration District: Carrick-on-Shannon
Death Country: Ireland
Volume: 8
Page: 48
FHL Film Number: 101582

Brother:
James Deignan
Estimated Birth Year: abt 1860
Date of Registration: 1865
Death Age: 5
Registration District: Carrick-on-Shannon
Death Country: Ireland
Volume: 3
Page: 57
FHL Film Number: 101582

From https://familysearch.org/
(Specific URLs subject to change)

However, Bridget had been diagnosed with an illness, "falling sickness." But she felt lucky she hadn't contracted consumption, as it was called. Irish country people used the term falling sickness to describe epilepsy, and treatments varied from community to community (MacLellan). In the workhouse where Bridget and her family lived, the treatment for children with falling sickness was shaving the child's head and placing leeches on the scalp. Leeches, it was believed, would suck out the poison that caused the sickness. Bridget had undergone this treatment so many times that she couldn't remember the number. The last time she'd received that particular treatment, just before her mother and sister died, her hair didn't grow back for a long time. When it did, it didn't grow back in the areas where the leeches had been allowed to stay for too long.

At one time, Bridget had lovely brown hair. She and her siblings would sometimes travel to the Killala Bay with their father and help him while he made extra money loading and unloading ships. Bridget and her sisters would wade out through the muddy beach loam into the salty water of the bay, even though it was cold, to wash their bodies and their hair. The salt water seemed to get rid of the lice, and it left them with a fresh ocean smell they all loved. The water was chilly, and they never used soap, but they would rub themselves with cut apples, especially their hair, if they could find some remaining after crates had been loaded. Grapes were the best, she insisted, but were much more difficult to find.

She and her sisters pretended to be *capaill bha* or kelpies, water horses that were magical and could transform themselves into beautiful women. These were beautiful snowy-white and ice-blue animals, muscular, and statuesque. They had flowing, curly manes that shone like prisms. They ruled the people in the towns around them, pronouncing decrees when they were women and snatching those who wouldn't heed when they were kelpies.

Mary washed Bridget's hair with softened castile soap and scrubbed her back with what she called a napkin, which was a kind of soft, cotton washcloth. Bridget felt pampered. The scent of the soap Mary brought to the jail reminded her of the soaps the Dayton family used when Bridget was a servant in their home before she began working for Dr. Coriell and his wife. Mrs. Coriell, Bridget said, used much more expensive soaps, the kind of soaps women in Philadelphia bought for their fancy powder rooms next to their exotic boudoirs. Mrs. Coriell always smelled of rose soap or herb soaps…goat's milk, lavender, lilac…and Bridget would sometimes wash her hands with these soaps. The scent was so strong that she could smell it for hours. But she'd never taken a plunge bath at Mrs. Coriell's home, nor had she ever taken a plunge bath at the Dayton house or anywhere else.

Bridget's life and that of her family had been difficult in the workhouse at Carrick-on-Shannon. Though Bridget was illiterate and uneducated, she knew the stories about how the workhouses had come to be. Many workhouses were built during the time of the Great Hunger because starvation and death were constant companions to the poor in both the towns and the countryside. The stone-covered walkways to these union workhouses were called the *casan na marbh* or "path of the dead" because so many people who entered died within the structures' shared, generic, and unsympathetic walls. The workhouse was just that, not a shelter, but a prison-like place where only the people who labored were fed. Men and women lived in separate quarters and children lived with their mothers when possible. When mothers were dead or missing, children became wards, and they were cared for in the female quarters or in the infirmary. Bridget had lived with her mother and sisters, working in most cases as a caregiver to orphaned children. She wasn't sure whether this was true of all the workhouses, but the Carrick-on-Shannon workhouse inmates saw an epidemic of consumption, or tuberculosis, in addition to famine fever.

When Mary Randolph left the Middlesex County jail after the first night she helped Bridget with her bath, she was troubled by the image of a child with a shaved head, lying in workhouse infirmary with leeches drawing blood from her scalp…a child in a room full of children dying of tuberculosis and fever, lice in their hair, if they had hair, and on their skin…older women hoping for an easy death, although that hope seemed irrelevant at that time. There were no easy deaths in the workhouse, not for the women and not for the children. The men's sickrooms were on the other end of the buildings, as the men and women, even husbands and wives, were kept apart. Brothers and sisters were kept apart. These were prisons for the old, the sick, and the dying. These were prisons for the poor and hopeless.

In March, Bridget told Mary about her brothers and sisters, the family farm in Sligo, and the appropriation of land by a landlord from London when her father had been unable to pay his debts. The family had been allowed to remain in their house on a small piece of the farm that they were sanctioned to cultivate. But the rest of the land had been divided up and rented to other families. Although the worst of the Great Hunger was over, many of the crops still suffered from the fungus that affected the potato. The land refused to yield crops as it had yielded them for previous generations. It was as though the land was rotting just as family life was rotting.

Bridget's father began to travel to the bay to earn money by loading and unloading ships there. When it was warm, it was not a difficult life for her father and his stronger children to go back and forth to the home where her mother stayed and worked small sections of land and grazed goats. But when it was cold, that was difficult. Near the bay, Bridget's father, Patrick, and her brothers and sisters would sleep wherever they could—in stables with horses, in storage warehouses, and sometimes on ships when the *seoltóiri*, sailors or captains, would let them. So many people who worked on the bay had that perpetual cough that brought up blood and paste; men would spit, neglectful of where and at whom. All the people near the water and the winds seemed to be sharing in some kind of swelling banshee cough.

Even after more than a year of working at the bay, Patrick and his children could not make enough money to pay their spring debts in May on what was called Gale Day. Gale Days were the first of May and the first of November, the traditional days when land rents were paid. When father and children returned to their home in Sligo during the second week in May, they found a "scalpeen," a roughly constructed shanty, leaning against the outside south wall of the house. Bridget's mother was inside with her youngest child, who was near death from fever. Patrick then gathered his wife and children and began petitioning workhouses for a place to shelter his family. These were not just places of destitution, though; they were places of spiritual poverty. They were places of unlimited hunger where marriages were broken, and brothers and sisters were separated. Old women and young women were thrown together, strangers sharing beds and bowls. The sick were placed in infirmary sickrooms where doctors, when available, practiced hopeful new cures, and sometimes patients died from those cures. Many doctors practiced herbal remedies, homeopathy, that had been a mainstay in Irish medicine for hundreds of years. But these herbal remedies had been practiced in rural areas where people lived apart, and there was time and space to heal. Some doctors at the workhouses still practiced bloodletting, and there were leeches, diuretics, laxatives, and all kinds of purgers for girls like Bridget who suffered from falling sickness.

Bridget's mother lived in fear that Bridget would be moved to the workhouse's idiot ward or a lunatic asylum, which was where young women with falling sickness or seizures were often placed. Sick children were sometimes taken away and never seen again—children with falling sickness, syphilitic children, children with lumps or bleeding illness, children who couldn't walk…they would disappear. So Bridget and her mother did their best to hide Bridget at times when the seizures took hold. Soon enough it was discovered. Bridget's head was shaved, and she was placed in a bed with another girl, also named Bridget, who had that banshee cough and died after a few days. The girl was buried in a mass grave, fourteen souls, in a cemetery field behind the workhouse. There were no gravestones, only long sequences of loose earth…

Bridget also spoke to Mary Randolph about the assorted and expensive purchases Mrs. Coriell would bring home from her trips to Philadelphia where she would stay in a posh hotel called the Continental with its Italian design and elevator. Mrs. Coriell described the shops she visited there: Alexander and Bush, where she bought the soft colored leather gloves she'd wear when it was cold, and for warmer days the embroidered silk and cotton *gants*, as she sometimes called them when they carried French labels. Mrs. Coriell loved French designers, and she'd spoken endlessly after her last trip to Philadelphia about a French designer and milliner called Caroline Reboux whose hats were being replicated and sold at Hunter's Hat Shop. She also loved an English designer named Charles Worth whose gowns were crafted in Paris. Mrs. Coriell owned at least ten elegant organdy dresses, silk fanchon and riding bonnets, shoes from DeHaven's, and boots from Fontaine's. Philadelphia boasted lavish perfume shops and one particularly sophisticated, fancy soap-making shop called Hitchings on North Seventh Avenue where Mrs. Coriell would buy the finest soaps and powders…olive oil Nabulsi soap, coconut oil, Savon de Marseille, sea salt soap, Aleppo, fruit soaps, flowers scents…

But Bridget was never jealous or resentful of Mrs. Coriell. She said she knew her place. She also described the women's books and magazines Mrs. Coriell would buy at a bookstore called Skelley's when she went to Philadelphia to shop or to see friends. And sometimes she would read from those magazines to her daughter when Mamey was having a difficult time sleeping. Mrs. Coriell would read to Mamey from nursery rhyme and fairytale books, but sometimes she became bored with those stories and would read from magazines about fashion, about soaps, and even about actors and actresses who frequented the playhouses of Philadelphia and New York City. There is a world, Bridget would say, that I only learned of listening to Mrs. Coriell read to her baby. She'd had no idea what beautiful women had to do to make themselves beautiful.

Mrs. Coriell enjoyed and appreciated one book writer in particular, a European dancer and actress named Lola Montez. Lola Montez was an exotic woman with a fascinating past, and Bridget knew all about her from the conversations she sometimes had with Mrs. Coriell when she helped her with her bath. When she washed Mrs. Coriell's hair for her, when she brought Mrs. Coriell fresh towels or fresh linens, when she helped her hang freshly washed curtains, Mrs. Coriell told the stories of Lola Montez's dazzling life. She told Bridget that Lola was descended from Spanish royalty, that she'd been a wonderful dancer and actress all throughout the theaters of Europe, entertained royal audiences with her dark, unconventional beauty, and that she'd stolen the hearts of men throughout Europe.

Bridget's Hanging

Lola was scandalous, having been married repeatedly, and some say never divorcing. She carried on shocking relationships with Franz Liszt as well as Alexandre Dumas. She later become romantically involved with King Ludwig I of Bavaria who, it was rumored, beheld her as she danced and asked her if her camisole was padded with fabric or if what he saw was her natural endowment. Lola responded by revealing her breasts to Ludwig and the rest of the noble audience in the chamber where she was performing. The king was taken with her beauty and outrageous behavior. He moved her into his palace and maintained her as his mistress, companion, and political adviser. The latter role actually hastened his downfall and eventual abdication.

Lola was unpopular in Bavaria because of her extravagant requests and the outrageousness of her public behavior. European newspapers reported that Lola demanded Bavarian citizenship and a noble title before she would again allow the king to share her bed. Against the counsel of his political allies, Ludwig submitted to her demands; she became Countess of Landsfeld, and she was granted a large financial endowment. Ludwig had several portraits of Lola painted. His favorite was hung in his Gallery of Beauties in his Bavarian palace. Their affair, Mrs. Coriell said, had so troubled his royal relatives that Lola had been threatened and forced to cross the Atlantic to the United States. In America, Lola reinvented herself as a writer and counselor for wealthy women who wished to remain beautiful or become beautiful. She wrote books and did interviews for magazines meant for the wealthiest society women in the United States. Mrs. Coriell read her books repeatedly. Skelley's Book Seller could not keep Lola's books on its shelves.

At first, Mary Randolph and Margaret Sullivan read to Bridget only from religious books or the Bible. They read the Gospels, the Psalms, and the story of Abraham and Isaac. Both Mary and Margaret loved the story of Isaac in the wilderness, sometimes called "the binding of Isaac." Both women employed the description of Isaac's deliverance to give Bridget hope for her own salvation.

And they came to the place which God had told him of; and Abraham built an altar there, and laid the wood in order, and bound Isaac his son, and laid him on the altar upon the wood.
And Abraham stretched forth his hand, and took the knife to slay his son.
And the angel of the LORD called unto him out of heaven, and said, Abraham, Abraham: and he said, Here *am* I.
And he said, Lay not thine hand upon the lad, neither do thou any thing unto him;
for now I know that thou fearest God…

Genesis 22:9–12

Abraham bound his son as a sacrifice…and Isaac was saved by an angel. Bridget, uneducated and illiterate, understood the meaning of their reading her the story repeatedly. It seemed everyone hoped she would be unbound from the noose, but the last thing she wanted was to be vindicated, found not guilty, or released from jail. Her days in the Middlesex County jail were the best of her life.

The Anglo-American Times

```
American Execution. Bridget Durgan, or Deignan,
a young woman, housemaid in the family of a phy-
sician, residing at New Market, in the state of
New Jersey, was executed at New Brunswick on the
30th for the murder of her mistress. It was a
cold-blooded murder, and no one seems to have had
any sympathy with her; the general expression
was that if anyone should be hung, she should.
The New York Times says, "Bridget was dressed
in a plain brown suit, and wore a white collar
and white gloves. The priests, the sheriff, and
```

any number of ex-sheriffs accompanied her, but she needed none of them. She was as steady as a ship's mast, and quite as devoid of emotion. The insulting expressions of the great, crushing crowd before her, their eager desire to be near her, the confusion of the moment, and the great fate before her would have unsettled the mind of any person; but she never moved a muscle, nor do we believe she cared the value of a half-penny. 'Don't let them Protestants know what I say,' said Bridget. The cap was drawn, the signal was given, the rope severed, and up she went with a jerk. In 30 minutes she was lowered into the coffin, and the cap was about to be removed, when the priest interposed to prevent it, it having been Bridget's request that her face should not be seen. The sheriff, however, insisted, and disclosed her pale, bloodless features to the people who gathered to look. As we have said, she made an exclusive grant of her last words to her Church. Several 'confessions' had been publically hawked about and offered for sale. It will seem strange, but it is nevertheless, true, that the Recorder of the City, Mr. David T. Jeffries, proposed to sell some time ago the confession of Bridget Durgan, and his modest price was $1000 in gold. Another man named Randolph, who, we believe, is a gaoler under Sheriff Clarkson, had a confession, and we understand his price was $250 gold or currency, we don't know which. One of the evening papers is reported to have paid $50 for another confession not worth the paper it's written on. Mr. Adrian, Bridget's counsel, furnished to the press still another confession, and the singular part of it all is that each holds all bogus but his own, and no two are alike."

September 1867

Bridget Deignan by Dean Duane

Two

Bridget's mother, sister, and two brothers died of tuberculosis in 1865 at the workhouse in Carrick-on-Shannon. They, too, were buried in unmarked graves in the long furrows of loose earth behind the workhouse infirmary. Bridget had been well enough to watch as her brother, James, was buried with two other children. She wanted to remember the location of his grave so that she'd be sure the rest of her family would be laid nearby, but she wasn't allowed to get close enough to be certain of the place. After her brother, Luke, sixteen and living in the men's section of the workhouse with his father, died and was buried, Patrick Deignan told his only surviving child, Bridget, that it was time for them to leave. He wanted to go back to Sligo before he died to climb a cairn, a pile of gravestones, on a hill called Knocknarea there. That spot is said to be the grave of Queen Medb or Maeve who ruled Ireland two thousand or so years before his birth. Like Bridget, Patrick Deignan was illiterate, but had grown up listening to the mythical stories of ancient Ireland.

Patrick's favorite tales had always revolved around Queen Maeve and her fierce ambition to survive in the world of more traditional rulers. Her most famous battle, the Tain Bo Cuailnge, was incited by a fortune competition between herself and her husband, who had appropriated some of her wealth—that is, her prize bull, when that bull refused to be owned by a woman. Maeve tried to procure a bull of equal significance called Donn Cuailnge, but instead she had to battle to obtain ownership. Although

Maeve and her forces lost the battle to a young hero named Cú Chulainn, Maeve was able to take ownership of the fabled bull, which she brought back to her home with her. Donn Cuailnge, the stolen bull, then killed her husband's celebrated bull and returned to his land to die of his wounds.

Legend has it that it is bad luck to take a stone from Maeve's grave and carry it away. When Patrick was a child, he'd visited the cairn under which Queen Maeve was supposedly buried, and he'd taken a stone and put it in his pocket; at that time, he didn't know about the belief that misfortune fell on those who took stones from the grave. A few weeks later, he'd heard the complete legend from his older sister who told him he'd probably angered the ghost of Queen Maeve. Patrick wanted to return the stone but had since lost track of it. He had spent all the years of his life since then wondering secretly if that stone and the angry ghost of Queen Maeve had cursed his life and that of his family, taking the lives of four of his infant children and the rest too young. Patrick convinced Bridget to help him get back to Sligo, to Knocknarea to apologize to the Queen's ghost and beg for the life of his one remaining child. Patrick was certain that if he could take a stone, any stone, up to the top of the cairn, he might save Bridget from her falling sickness. There was a Poor Law Union workhouse in Sligo that had been too crowded to admit Patrick and his family a few years earlier, but he was convinced that he should die in Sligo, perhaps in that workhouse, after he'd delivered his "remorse" stone to the ghost.

Bridget and her father left Carrick-on-Shannon in late March of 1866 on foot. They were able to beg a ride from a teamster carrying livestock to a large farm outside Glennagoolagh. They slept that night in the bed of the wagon after the driver returned to his home in Drumiskabole. Late the next night they arrived at the workhouse in Sligo where Patrick was received. Although assisted emigration—that is, an organized program wherein the poor and illiterate of Ireland had their transportation/emigration fees paid by the British government, absentee landlords, philanthropists and/or Union Poor Law workhouses—had lost approval, the

Bridget's Hanging

Poor Law Unions continued to provide funds for destitute individuals who wanted to emigrate through 1890, especially to females (Moran). Because workhouses were refuges for widows and children, there was no place for Bridget, as their women's accommodations were over maximum capacity. Sligo had some emigration funds available, and her father convinced the administrators or guardians to pay Bridget's fare to Liverpool and then to America. Bridget didn't want to leave her father, but he convinced her that as soon as he returned a stone, any stone, to Queen Maeve's cairn, his family curse would be lifted, and Bridget's life would be transformed. She had great hopes as she left her dying father to catch a boat to Liverpool. It doesn't seem that Patrick ever made it back to Maeve's grave.

This is an excerpt from *Life, Crimes, and Confession of Bridget Durgan*, written by the Rev. Mr. Brendan, a man who had only once briefly conversed with Bridget, published for an impressive sum of money just after her death on the gallows. This false confession was marketed as though Bridget had penned it herself. Bridget, however, was unable to read or write.

BRIDGET'S EARLY LIFE.

In my prison cell in the town of New Brunswick, I am sitting all alone tonight. Alone, did I say? No! no! not alone! Not alone! For all round me flit spectres of darkness and woe. They shake their shadowy fingers in my face, and whisper to me that there is no reprieve! No pardon! I must be hung tomorrow. Hung! It must be an awful death to be hung! To have a rope put around my neck, to be choked, and have my neck broken, and then dangle down there in the prison yard like an old cat. That is dreadful to be hung that way! But I do not believe there is any chance for my escape.

Everybody is very bitter against me; especially these Jersey people. It makes no difference to them that I am a woman. They are very hard-natured folks. But there is no use in my feeling a bit angry at them. No! for I will be hung certain, and it will make me feel better if I make a true confession. I will write it out now, and give it to Mr. Brendan; as he is the only one I think anything of at all. I am not friendly to these newspaper fellows; for they set everybody down on me. I will give this to Mr. Brendan before I leave this cell to go to the gallows down in the yard tomorrow. Now, dear Mr. Brendan, with my dying, solemn voice I will write it down, as I cannot speak it, that all the other confessions I have made were false. People used to bother me so that I would tell them everything that came into my head, just for the fun of it. But I am past all that now, and what I am going to write about my miserable life and my crimes is true every whit. And with my last breath I will ask you to publish it to the world, and show young people the danger of going into wrong ways in their youth.

I was born in the village of Duncliffe, County Sligo, Ireland, in 1843; and was raised in pretty good circumstances, at least for this station in life occupied by my family. My childhood, up to twelve years of age, was passed in my native village of Duncliffe; and then it was resolved by my father and mother, to put me out to service in the household of a gentleman, who lived close by.

Bridget's Hanging

There I continued to live for about three years; when a circumstance occurred, that shaped my after life in the channel which has led me now to this disgrace of dying on the gallows. There was a May day party given, and as I was taken along with the family to help to wait on them, I was thus thrown into the company of James, the son of my employer. He had always been very attentive to me, but on this day he was particularly so; and before the close of the excursion he invited me to take a stroll with him into a piece of woodland nearby. He was so kind and merry, that I soon forgot all else than the pleasure of being with him.

But there is no need to repeat a tale so common, and so often heard. Afterwards, when I found what had become of me, I resolved to leave Ireland and come to America, where I would be known by nobody. As may be supposed, I was furnished with money to come out here by parties, who were only too glad to be rid of me at so small an expense. In the regular time I arrived here and hired myself out to do housework. But, after I had been at my place for a few months, my mistress, making a discovery, would not keep me any longer, but turned me out of the house.

From that moment I began to hate everybody; but most of all my mistresses; and I resolved to kill someone if the chance only came in my way.

I wandered about till at last I got into a shelter. Some weeks after that I was free on account of getting rid of my incumberance. This was in New York; and one day as I was walking along the street, I met a woman named Ellen Gilroy, who spoke to me and asked me if I were not in trouble. I told her that I was, and then she said she had seen me one day up at the asylum where I had been, and where she had also been doing some cleaning.

"What do you expect to do now? Asked she.

"I don't know," said I, "but I'd do most anything to get along."

"You don't mean to work, do you? says she.

"Yes," says I, "I want to find a place."

"Why, that's all nonsense! What's the use of your going to work when you'd be turned out in a day or two, or just soon as you are found out. You come with me, and I'll show you how to get along without that!"

I did not care what I did; nor what became of me; and away I went with Ellen Gilroy. She took me to a tenement house in the lowest part of the city, and there I stayed for about three weeks, doing just that she and the rest of the women there did.

One night the police came down to the house, about twelve o'clock at night to arrest one of us for robbing a man. Being fearful that they intended to take me, I jumped out of the second story back window, got into an alley that ran behind a fence, and escaped, although the police were standing all around the house. I walked about the street the whole of that night, and in the morning went over to Brooklyn. There I made a resolution to do better, and get a place if I could. At last, I made a bargain with a woman who sold fish, to help her for two dollars a week.

I behaved very well for some time, and finally got into Mr. Dolan's family to do the housework. There I lived about three months, when I left and took service with a Mrs. Horning. She and I did not agree very well, and one day she ordered me to leave; and called me a devilish infernal slut. This roused my blood, and I went up to my room, with the full determination to kill both her and her sister, who had also treated me badly.

Life, Crimes, and Confession of Bridget Durgan
By Rev. Mr. Brendan

Analysis of the text and its contents proves that the details presented are as counterfeit as some of the scientific testimony in Bridget's hastily commenced trial. Research has proven that Brendan's account, although believed by much of the paying public, was totally fabricated.

Brendan's account of Bridget's early life described her as a young woman who grew up in a financially secure situation who left her comfortable existence in Ireland because she became pregnant by the son of her employer. She traveled to New York City, where she aborted her child and became a prostitute, eventually running from the law and hiding as a housemaid, where she seduced the husbands and adult sons of her mistresses. Eventually, she became so filled with hate that her humanity was destroyed, and she became a murderous animal.

As interesting as this tale might be, none of the facts of Bridget's life corroborate it. The entire confession is a compendium of imaginative misrepresentations from newspaper articles and local gossip. In fact, as soon as newspapers began printing any information about Mrs. Coriell's murder, misinformation was also being printed, and the more salacious and explicit, the more interested the public became. Clearly, Brendan's motive for creating an incredibly detailed and completely fraudulent confession was money. Americans purchased his text because it was sensational, and because America believed that an illiterate, "Roman" (Catholic), immigrant servant girl was an immoral, heartless murderer who was willing to tell the truth of her sinful life only to relative stranger, a Protestant man who derided her religion and her faith, and who was convinced that she was a cold-blooded killer. This makes little sense.

Nativism is sometimes called a sociopolitical ideology, but it is in this case better defined as a "feeling" among members of a society, encouraged by the media and political speech, that rejects people from unfamiliar places with different beliefs or practices. On some level, this occurs in every culture, but during the nineteenth century in the United States, nativism was severe. Historically, the European-descended, "recognized" society was predominantly white, Anglo-Saxon Protestant who, in general, either tolerated or embraced the concept of racial superiority. For members of this society, "whiteness" was defined not only by skin color but by practice and religious beliefs. Catholics, who were referred to as "Romans," were associated with the concepts of medieval social repression, papal despotism, and the kind of spiritual ignorance wherein people worshipped idols and churches sold indulgences. Further, immigrants as a general rule came to the United States during this time with little or nothing in order to escape economic and religious oppression. These were poor people in threadbare clothing who came off "coffin ships" sick and sometimes near death, requiring charity care and charity housing. Immigrants, especially the Irish, were uneducated and unskilled. They brought with them poverty, crime, and disease, according to the Protestant respectable classes (Billington).

As early as 1806, Roman Catholics were not allowed to hold public office in many states because, according to nativist beliefs, allegiance to a pope was allegiance to a theocratic monarch and thus un-American. President John Adams saw the influence of the Roman church as antiliberty and antidemocracy. Many elected officials saw Catholic immigration as a kind of foreign invasion that threatened the very fundamentals of Protestant American values. Two very influential sociopolitical leaders, Lyman Beecher and Samuel Morse, were vehemently anti-Catholic and anti-immigrant. Beecher was a Presbyterian minister and Protestant social leader whose anti-Catholic sermons incited the burning of a Catholic convent near Boston. Morse was an anti-immigration activist, a defender of slavery as a benevolent institution, and an opponent of what he called the Catholic menace. In his book *Foreign Conspiracy Against the Liberties of the United States,* Morse wrote that "popery" was an absolute and tyrannical political system that had as its objective the appropriation of America's religious freedom and the development of a theocracy. The pope was working toward the achievement of these objectives, according to Morse, by flooding the borders with immigrants from Catholic countries. A parlor game called "Break the Pope's Neck" was apparently popular in parts of the country. Into this climate came Bridget Deignan.

Brendan's text, including his fictional "confession," which he presented as being from the pen of Bridget Deignan, included the following epilogue:

```
           Bridget's Imprisonment.
There have been numbers of various accounts given
in the papers of the conduct of Bridget Durgan
during the time of her imprisonment previous to
```

her execution. From among these it was almost impossible to obtain an authentic and reliable narrative as each of them purported to be the only veritable one. But from all the sources at command we publish the following, which we believe to be entirely correct; as it comports in every essential particular with her own narrative and confession.

During the first few days of her prison life she exhibited exactly the same traits that a wild beast would have done. Her eyes glared wildly; she would clutch her hands in the air, tug furiously at her straggling hair, rush from one side of the cell to the other, throw herself on her straw bed and bite it with her teeth.

The last act was a favorite one of hers and it proved very conclusively her guilt at least circumstantially; for the neck of her victim was bitten nearly through on one side.

But the dreary solitude of the narrow room with its barred window and strong, impassable door, and the stolid, stern face of the keeper, who alone gave her her food, reduced her to tameness. Yet even then the brutal part of her harsh nature was still predominant. She would crouch down, half sitting and half lying on her bed and leer up whenever the door was opened.

Her case being a peculiarly atrocious one she had not been in prison many days before she was almost besieged by philanthropically disposed ladies and gentlemen some of whom would even bring children with them. Of course as Christians we would never object to religions and well disposed people visiting the miserable inmates of a prison and endeavoring to mitigate the horrors of confinement; but we do think that latterly there has come to be too much of maudlin sympathy, as well as excitement in regard to these matters.

The more desperate and wicked the criminal is and the more deplorably wicked is his or her offense, the greater number of those well-disposed but unthinking people flock to the cell to offer consolation and direct the mind to heaven. And the natural goodness of their hearts causing them to pity the culprit, they generally take with them little presents of sweetmeats or segars or tobacco, as prison fare is so hard.

Such a mistaken course is in reality most injuries upon society. For there is always a class too ignorant and vicious to rise to distinction by good or great deeds; and yet being ambitious, they turn to crime to thereby become notorious. We recollect ourselves a case of a young girl, handsome, of respectable parentage, and with a fine intellect, who deliberately sought the acquaintance of a libertine in order that she might be seduced, and thereby get her name up in the criminal paper. And while her parents and friends were bewailing the disgrace and ruin brought upon her and her family she eagerly bought the paper containing the account

> of her own sin, and the likeness of herself and the villain, she actually gloried in showing the paper to parties who came to the house.
> So with Bridget Durgan. When she found what an excitement her hideous crime had caused and began to be visited by the philanthropists we have mentioned, instead of her thoughts being diverted from the things of earth and directed to the awful future into which she was so soon to be ushered, they were intensely fastened on earthly matters. How she looked when the visitors came was a matter of much moment to her and what people said outside, whether they abused her much or little, and what they thought &c. was also of the deepest interest or her.
>
> Life and Crimes of Bridget Durgan, 43–4

Brendan's murder pamphlet paints two contradictory images of Bridget. These images are also different from many of the descriptions of her printed in most newspapers and editorials. Brendan describes her as a bloodthirsty murderer at one point, but later as a self-aware human being with the moral capacity to forgive those individuals preparing to hang her and those involved in her prosecution. She is described as a caged animal, "tamed" only by the lone face of her jailer…yet he also stresses that philanthropists begin to speak with and counsel her within days in the performance of their Christian duty.

Brendan writes two different stories, apparently to appeal to two different types of readers, perhaps in the hope that both will buy his pamphlet. Further, Brendan proclaims that these philanthropists, who, in sympathy and for their love of God, bring prayer and gifts to "miserable inmates" are in fact doing a disservice to society as a whole. He defines Bridget as a member of "a class too ignorant and vicious" to respond spiritually or gratefully to small kindnesses. But Brendan expects his readers to see him as the one person to whom she grants the truth of her tale on the evening before she is hanged. There is little sense in his version of events.

Further, the proven facts of the case conflict with his fabrication. Again, Bridget had not grown up in a middle-class family in Ireland; she did not leave Ireland pregnant with the child of her employer's son; she did not work as a prostitute in New York City; as ill as she was, she would not have been able to jump fences while evading a vice arrest. Bridget arrived in New York City on June 7, 1866, just days before she began working for the Dayton family in New Jersey.

This is the cover of Brendan's published pamphlet as it appeared for sale in 1867:

Although it's unclear where Brendan "found" the details he chose for his text, he was not the originator of the notion of "Bridget Durgan as caricature villain." The creative remaking of Bridget Deignan's life had

Bridget's Hanging

begun almost as soon as ink was spilled on newsprint about the murder of Mrs. Coriell. For example, the *Boston Herald*, in its reporting of this case on February 28, 1867, two days after the murder, contrasted Bridget's "moral ugliness" to the "uncommon beauty and suavity of manners" possessed by Mrs. Coriell. Bridget is described in such terms as "a cunning evil doer," "half idiot," and as a "half-witted creature."

> Bridget Durgan, the alleged murderess, has an evil look that strikes a person forcibly on beholding her. Her manner throughout the inquest betokened that she was either a cunning evil doer, hiding her moral ugliness under a simulated appearance of half idiot, or was a half-witted creature in the full sense of the word. The un-fortunate victim of the murder, Mrs. Mary Ellen Coriell, was aged about twenty-five, a woman of uncommon beauty and suavity of manners. She was regarded by the citizens of Newmarket as a person whose gentle nature and goodness of heart were sufficient of themselves to make her loved and respected by all who knew her.
>
> *Boston Herald* 28 February 1867

One day after the murder, several newspapers, including the *National Republican*, published in Washington, DC, printed that Bridget had made a full confession to the murder (see chapter 1). The story of her "full confession" was published in the *Boston Journal*, *Boston Traveler*, and the *Daily National Intelligencer*, including many others. One newspaper, the *Evening Star*, published in Washington, DC, even printed a short editorial about how American freedoms have encouraged women to commit murder, citing the female murderer of Mrs. Coriell as one example. These assertions that Bridget was indeed guilty of the murder imprinted on the public psyche long before the trial began.

For example, the following article was published in the *New York Times* just weeks after Mrs. Coriell's murder.

```
FEMALE CRIMINALS.-Why is it that there are so
many murders perpetrated in this country nowa-
days by women! It is not a great while since
Mr. Burroughs was killed in Washington by Mary
Harris. It is only a few weeks since Mollie
Trussell shot to death the man whose name she
bore in Chicago. A fortnight since, the ser-
vant woman, Bridget Durgan, stabbed and killed
her mistress at Newmarket, N.J. On Friday last,
Emma Howard stabbed to the heart a young man
named Sparr, in Chicago. And beside these actu-
al murders, there have within a few months been
half-a-dozen attempts at murder by women, which
have been frustrated by one circumstance or
another. It might be worthy of thought whether
the impunity which women enjoy in this country
of doing men to death has not something to do
with this shocking state of affairs. It is true
that Mrs. GRENDEL was executed for her butcher-
ies in Pittsburgh a couple years ago, but this
was an exceptional case. As a rule, murderesses
are acquitted with triumph.
                                  13 March 1867
```

Three

Bridget arrived in Liverpool, England, in May 1866 after having been granted free passage with a dozen or so other women from Sligo as human ballast on a coal ship carrying a light load. From there, Bridget purchased passage on a bark, a three-masted sailing ship, called the *Orient*. The following are the title page and three of the sixteen-page passenger list/ship manifest from the *Orient*'s voyage May/June 1866. The manifest closes with the statement, "769 souls."

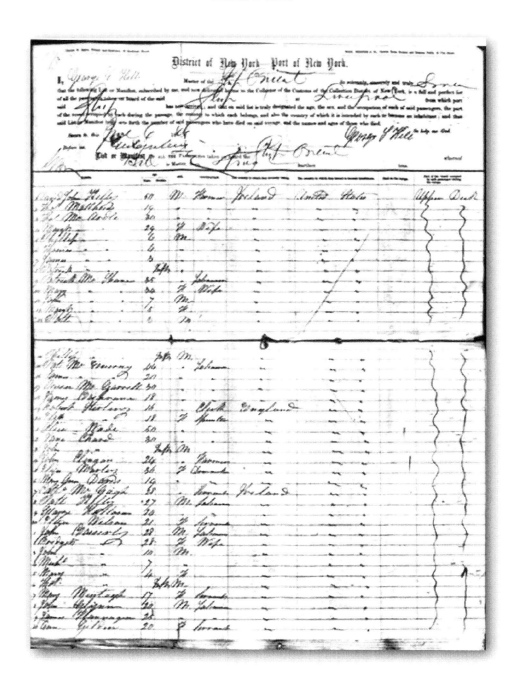

Bridget's Hanging

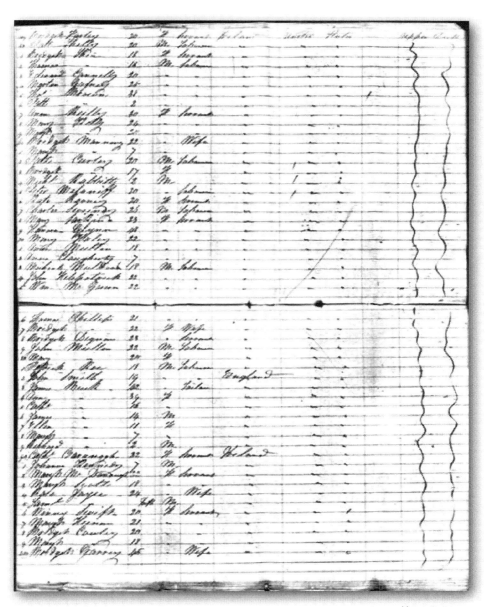

See line #8, sheet 2

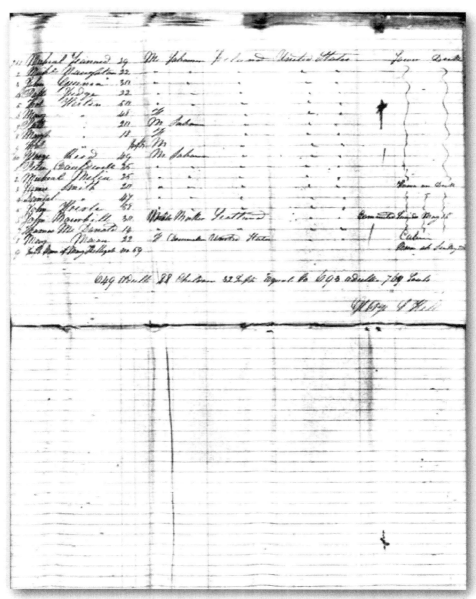

Bridget's Hanging

The *Orient*, a bark, was a sailing vessel that is considered minuscule when viewed through a twenty-first-century eye. The term "bark" is derived from Latin and means small boat. The *Orient*, like other sailing ships of that time, organized passengers in classes: first class or quarter deck passage, which was, as it is today, replete with exclusive, comfortable stateroom accommodations often compared to luxury hotel rooms. A first-class saloon was available only to passengers of this class, even on a ship as small as the *Orient*. Second-class upper-deck accommodations on barks, though not as nice as first class, included cabins with beds and some level of privacy; second-class passengers usually dined separately from steerage or third-class passengers who were usually given their rations on the orlop deck or in their shared steerage compartment. Both first- and second-class passengers were offered time on the deck to recreate without the presence of steerage passengers who traveled without privacy in a portion of the ship near the steerage mechanisms.

The third-class passengers were often restricted to their single, hollow compartment or hold whose bulkheads were lined with what is tantamount to wooden shelving berths. Families brought to the ship small rugs or shawls on which to sleep, or they slept on whatever clothing they brought with them on their long ocean voyage. There were no comforts provided to these passengers, only the minimum of food and water. And it was, interestingly, the men and women who'd lived in the Poor Law workhouse system who fared best in steerage class. Workhouse life had prepared its inmates, like Bridget, to adapt to congested living spaces, survive on minimal servings of food, and conform to restricted schedules. Bridget felt comfortable among the mothers and children in steerage; between her long days in the infirmary at Carrick-on-Shannon, she'd worked as a caregiver to the children whose mothers were ill or overwhelmed by their grim situations—separated from husbands and sons by workhouse structures, from extended family by poverty, and from stability by social conditions. In fact, steerage was very much like workhouse life.

Just as the population aboard the ship was a microcosm of society with its rich first-class men and women being catered to by the ship's stewards, entertained by its sailors, and charmed by one another's stories of money and property, the penury class was kept from their midst by solicitous pursers, deck mates, and assistants. And just as in society now, there was at that time among the second class some young men who'd lost ownership of first-class status through laziness, impiety, or alcoholism. These young men were at that time called "remittance" men, boys from wealthy families who'd become embarrassments to their banker fathers or landowning grandfathers. They'd been expelled from colleges or forced out of medical internships, law apprenticeships, or engineering training programs. They were disappointments to the mothers who once doted on them and the connected young women whose fathers saw them as potential sons-in-law. These idlers were referred to as "remittance men" because every few months, softhearted mothers or grandmothers would remit to them just enough money to maintain their lives away from home, away from the prying eyes of society peers whose successful sons and grandsons were not embarrassments. Second-class accommodations were peppered with young men traveling "overseas" to no particular destination. They were often escorted from barks and ships at foreign ports because of their drunken or aggressive behaviors. There were more than ten such young men on the *Orient* in May/June 1866, three of whom from Germany were dangerously aggressive.

Margaret Sullivan listened to and was touched by Bridget's story, that is, the real description of her early life. She'd seen Bridget many times in the village of New Market and noticed that Bridget was shy, quiet, always averted her eyes and appeared modest. And although Bridget was a Catholic, Margaret sensed she was a good Christian girl. Margaret had grown up with a minister father who'd always said, "Catholics are often devout Christians corrupted by an unnatural fondness for statues." As soon as Bridget had been arrested, Margaret went to the jail to try to speak to her to find out whether she was guilty of murder or a victim of her gender, her Romanism, or her illiteracy. Margaret was sensitive to Bridget's status as an Irish immigrant because her father had come to America and had faced some of the same nativist difficulties.

    Margaret had begun teaching Bridget to read by schooling her in the alphabet. Although writing the letters was difficult for her, she learned the letter names and had started to learn the letter sounds. Margaret brought in a copy of a teaching book called *John Brown, Hero*. The book was written specially to teach children to read, as it was written in easily decodable words. It was also written to introduce children to reform ideas about the evil of the institution of slavery, which had recently been ended by the Thirteenth Amendment, and the equity of all men under God. The words were small and followed a simple rhyme scheme.

> John Brown, hero, heard the voice of the Lord;
> In his hands he took a just and holy sword…

Margaret never revealed to Bridget that she was the author of the book. In fact, she wrote on the paper cover of her copy, "This book written by Rev. Joseph Hope for the purpose of instructing God's children."

    Like Bridget, Margaret lived in a world where women were socially insignificant and had no voice in government or culture. Margaret, although certainly not rich, had not grown up in poverty like Bridget. Her father was an Irish Protestant who worked as a stonemason until he married her mother, the daughter of a Lutheran preacher. She was raised as a Lutheran and was educated by her mother and grandparents. Margaret grew up in the house where her mother had grown up with her grandparents, her mother, her four brothers, and most of the time her father, who attended seminary in Gettysburg, Pennsylvania, on and off for several years.

    Margaret had begun her teaching career at eleven years old, teaching the Gospel to children younger and older than she. She hoped one day to get married, but wanted to marry someone whom she could call a reformer, a man of principle, a man of God. Margaret was lovely, but played down her large blue eyes and light-brown hair by tightly braiding her hair and pinning it up or wearing a snood or simple hairnet. She was modest and preferred to wear clothing that was a shade of brown or gray. Black, she believed, was too dramatic, and pastels and bright colors were too eye-catching.

Bridget struggled to sound letters into words, so she would often ask Margaret to read to her. Though she loved Bible stories, she asked Margaret and Mary Randolph again if they had any journals or magazines such as *Godey's Lady's Book* and *Peterson's Magazine*. Bridget told them again about Lola Montez. She said Mrs. Coriell once told her the story of Lola's mother crossing the Atlantic and Indian Oceans to bring young Lola, fifteen at the time, from England back to India to meet her future husband, a sixty-year-old Indian Supreme Court justice named Sir Abraham Lumley. Lola's mother returned to England on the *Orient*, the same ship (or so the story was told) that had brought Bridget to America, to Castle Garden, to the United States. Lola, descended from Spanish royalty, provocative dancer, actress, bigamist, and mistress to King Ludwig I of Bavaria, Bridget stressed, had written countless articles about beauty and femininity.

Bridget remembered and quoted from Mrs. Coriell's favorite text, *The Arts of Beauty; Or, Secrets of a Lady's Toilet* by Madame Lola Montez:

```
Neither the buona roba of the Italians, nor the
linda of the Spaniards, nor the embonpoint of
the French, can fully reach the mystical stan-
dard of beauty to the eye of American taste.
And if I were to say that it consists of an
indescribable combination of all these, still
you would go beyond even that, before you would
be content with the definition. Perhaps the
best definition of beauty ever given, was by a
```

Bridget's Hanging

```
French poet, who called it a certain je ne sais
qwoi, or, I don't know what !
```
(20)

Bridget smiled shyly as she told Mary and Margaret that she didn't really understand the passage or the foreign language words, but Mrs. Coriell had understood. Mrs. Coriell was "American" beautiful. Bridget thought it would be nice to be "American" pretty.

Both Mary and Margaret found it surprising and a bit unnerving that Bridget, awaiting trial for the murder of Mary Ellen Coriell, talked so pleasantly about Mrs. Coriell's fascination with Lola Montez, with Lola's eccentricities, affairs, and indignities. In fact, Bridget retold Lola's life story with a girlish laugh, as though she'd forgotten that Mrs. Coriell was dead, and she stood accused of her murder. There was a foolishness, a disconnect with the reality of her situation as she described King Ludwig's Gallery of Beauties to them. And for a moment, both Mary and Margaret saw Bridget as a woman who, just for a moment, might have committed a murder as she ventured from the real and melancholy world of New Market, New Jersey, to the exotic and passionate fantasy universe of a glamorous international dancer, actress, and mistress to wealthy, influential men…just for a moment.

The prosecutor in Middlesex County, New Jersey, Mr. Charles Herbert, insisted to the news reporters who'd descended upon New Brunswick after the murder of Mary Ellen Coriell that Bridget Deignan murdered Mrs. Coriell in the hope of replacing her in the life and heart of her husband, Dr. Coriell. Neither Mary nor Margaret had seen any indication that Bridget had an attachment to Dr. Coriell, although she did speak often of his young daughter, Mamey. But after listening to Bridget excitedly talk about Franz Liszt and Alexandre Dumas…about portrait galleries, elopements, and Bavarian nobility, they began to wonder, if only for that single moment, whether there wasn't some deep, clandestine layer to this simple, swollen, childish woman who seemed insensible to the fact that she was facing a murder trial, a trial that would determine whether she would live or die. But Bridget was infantile in many ways and lacked the insight to understand her situation. She also lacked, they decided, the malice to have murdered her mistress.

When Bridget boarded the *Orient* in Liverpool in May of 1866, she'd never heard of Lola Montez or Liszt or Dumas, and she didn't know at that time that the *Orient*, the same ship she boarded, had played a role in the life of Lola Montez. All she knew at that time was that her father promised the pall that had hung over her family for all the years of her life would cease to exist once he replaced a stone on the cairn of Queen Maeve. In her mind, her long ocean crossing became a kind of magical voyage like the "imramha" told by her father, stories about heroes journeying to the land of spirits, landing on the shores of the otherworld or the realm of the dead. Bridget's father would tell his children stories as they walked or, if lucky, rode to the bay to work the ships. He described the otherworld as a perfect place where it was always summer and life was forever easy. He sometimes referred to this mystic land as the Isle of the Blest where enchanted animals lived idyllic lives, handfed by the noble girls and boys who found their way to such a piece of heaven. As Bridget boarded the *Orient* and began her passage to America, in her mind she heard her father's voice telling her that when she began her journey to the Isle of the Blest, she should watch for the numinous ball of thread or clew. She should follow it as it unwound because that would be the sign that her magical journey had begun, that she would soon find a kind of heaven. And that's what she did and what she believed.

The Isle of the Blest is an otherworldly island described generally in the myths of multiple cultures, including Greek, Norse, Indian, etc. The ball of thread, or clew, also runs through the myths of multiple cultures, most notably the story of Theseus and his escape from the labyrinth in which he was supposed to die as a sacrifice to the Minotaur. Theseus saved himself by binding the loose end of the clew at the entrance of the labyrinth, killing the Minotaur, and then escaping by following the thread to his freedom. The Celtic version of this legend is described in written mythology as early as the seventh century in the Book of Leinster. Though neither Bridget nor her father could read, the stories circulated like nursery rhymes in urban and rural areas. The most common Irish version of the story, the Voyage of Bram, tells of a young man named Bram who is invited to the Otherworld, sometimes called the Isle of the Blest or the Land of the Young, by mysterious music that hypnotizes him. He travels with companions over the sea to this magic place and lands where there are beautiful women who invite him to live for a thousand years without illness or the troubles of age or hunger. The young men stay there for a time, but some grow restless and want to return to the old world. The people of the island warn the travelers there is only one place where age and illness cannot trouble them. The queen of the Isle of Women throws her magic clew to the travelers and pulls them back to her supernatural island.

The concept of the Isle of the Blest and the transcendent clew whose thread offers escape and sanctuary are obviously symbols to which most immigrants cling when they leave their homes. For someone like Bridget Deignan who was leaving a country that not only failed her economically and medically, but also spiritually, the magical thinking that prompted her to board a ship first to Liverpool and then New York City promised her that she would not be hanged in August of 1867.

The first few days Bridget spent on the *Orient* were breezy and cool, but the sun was warm, and she enjoyed spending time on the deck looking out over the Atlantic Ocean. The reflection of the sun's rays off the rolling waves was blinding at times, and she occasionally became light-headed from the brilliance and the rocking of the ship on the pitches and swells. But the fresh air, as cool as it was, offered a welcome relief from the stale atmosphere in steerage. Bridget was aware that she could still be affected by her falling disease, that she might become faint and lose consciousness on deck. She was afraid she might be marked as a liability to her new country as she disembarked in New York City and might, as a consequence, be sent back to Ireland. But somewhere in her mind was the authentic belief that once Queen Maeve was appeased, she would find herself free from the falling disease, that her lovely brown hair would return, and she would live a life as other American women lived. She believed she would find a home in New York, marry, and bear many children…as long as her father could keep his promise.

A little German boy named Willie was traveling on the ship with family members: first and second cousins. He was about four years old and was often without supervision. Bridget shared her water rations with him beginning the second day of the trip because he was always thirsty. She had taken him into her heart, as he seemed lonely and so dissimilar to everyone else on board. Even in her simplicity, Bridget saw in Willie something she recognized in herself, an irregularity, a jarring peculiarity. Just as Bridget spent hours during the first week aboard looking out across the Atlantic, Willie would stand on a small crate next to her and in mixed German and English, talk about the "nixy." A nix or nixy is a German fairy-tale creature about which parents tell their children to frighten them away from dangerous waterways. Nixes are like mermaids in that they're part fish and part human. However, they can be male or female, can become invisible, and they are prophetic. Parents tell children that nixes hide themselves near rivers and oceans in order to abduct boys and girls, bring them to their underwater palaces, and drown them. Although Bridget understood little of Willie's story about the nix, she asked one of the German women in steerage what a nix was and why a little boy might fear one.

Like Bridget, Willie was not well. There were quite a few people on the *Orient* who were suffering from the flux, or dysentery, which was common during ocean travel at that time. Water was collected and often stored in open barrels; cleanliness was subject to the availability of water. Seasickness contributed to the duration and severity of the flux, as the nausea from the ship's rocking caused vomiting and weakness. Willie was sometimes both seasick and suffering from the flux. He was very thin with exceedingly pale, white skin and dark circles around his eyes. Willie quickly became disinterested in eating, regularly shivered from the cold, and was often thirsty. In the sunlight, Bridget could see purplish bruising on his skin and noticed the hollows in his cheeks deepening. Within days, Willie was becoming weaker and was moving around the ship less and less. He started spending most of his time in the steerage compartment on the berth where his cousin maintained her two children. On a Sunday morning, Bridget checked on Willie, who seemed insentient; his body was cold. On Monday morning, he was dead.

    Bridget had seen children die while living at the workhouse, but this death seemed different to her. The children who died in the workhouse died in the infirmary close to at least a few people who hoped for their recovery. On Monday before noon, Willie was wrapped in an old rug, which the sailors secured with a heavy chain that served as a weight. The weight caused the body to sink and quelled mariner superstitions about ghosts and the splash of the corpse in sea burials. One sailor whispered a short prayer in German, and Willie was dropped from the side of the ship; his cousin stood by briefly and then returned to the steerage compartment. Bridget watched as Willie's small, trussed body sank into the Atlantic, and she noticed that threads from the rug that were loose remained on the surface as the rest of his slight form floated downward. She felt confused... she imagined Willie, even in death afraid, being dragged to the nix's underwater palace to be drowned, but still she watched the threads from his shroud floating on the surface of the softly rolling water...remembering the ball of thread unwinding in her father's description of the Isle of the Blest. What was at play? she asked herself. Disoriented by her own inability to understand, she thought of Willie's fear of the nixes and their ability to prophesize…what had they been foretelling? A little boy's death? She tried to separate that confusion from the hopeful omen of the thread, rolling and unwinding on the surface of the Atlantic Ocean, portending her own good fortune. How can that sign be promising when someone very like herself, an outsider, had just been dropped, cold and stiff, off the side of the ship that was, by virtue of her father's promise, carrying her to a place not unlike heaven?

Bridget had never been able to understand the day-to-day operations of the world and its citizens. So few thoughtful things had ever made sense to her that she'd stopped asking why, even in prayer. After she'd watched her brother James buried in the workhouse graveyard, she'd paused for one moment and asked God, "Why do these things happen?" That was the first and last time she'd asked that question for as long as she remembered. And she'd asked it expecting no answer. But after her father told her about his theft of the stone from the grave of the goddess queen, she began to believe just as he'd explained it…a malevolence had befallen his family. His recklessness was to blame for everything amiss. Things had started to make some sense to her: Maeve's curse had somehow obstructed the benevolence that God would have showered on her family if God had been able to circumvent Maeve's malediction. Bridget watched the threads on the ocean's surface unwind as she hoped her father had lived up to his promise and returned that stone. Maybe he hadn't done it yet, and that's why Willie had died…maybe he would do it that day or the next.

Bridget spent that evening in the steerage compartment of the ship lying on the left end of a berth with a mother and daughter who were suffering nausea from the ocean travel. After Willie's death and burial, she was certain she would be affected by her falling sickness. She stayed on the berth all night, finding herself in and out of "slumbers," which is what her mother called the aftereffect of her seizures. If she could keep to her place until she was certain her father had kept his promise, she knew no one on

Bridget's Hanging

the ship would know she had falling sickness, and she could begin her new life. But life on the *Orient* wasn't so simple. Food and water were distributed to the steerage class passengers on the deck morning and evening. Body waste buckets were on deck, and on windless days the air in steerage became hard to breathe.

Nighttime was the most difficult, as sleeping men stunk from drinking and smoking, children needed changing, and berths were filled to capacity and sometimes beyond. There were nights when Bridget slept on the compartment's floor because of crowding, and she'd find herself wanting to walk the deck to alleviate her stiffness. If she heard men's voices as she climbed to the deck, she would return to the compartment; if she didn't, she would move quietly to the port side of the ship, lean her head and shoulders over the water, inhale deeply and pray that her father had kept his promise.

Four nights after Willie's death, Bridget leaned on the bulwark and listened to the sound of the water. She could hear the subdued voices of men from the bridge, but everything else was quiet. Within a few minutes, a man approached her, a remittance man, she believed, speaking German. She was startled but cordial and told him that she knew no German. He smelled of brandy, an apple brandy that many of the second-class passengers drank, of stale smoke, and fish. He fell against her and laughed, saying something in German. Bridget understood two of his words, ozean and frauen (ocean and women). He grabbed both her arms, and she struggled to get away. Bridget woke the next morning on the floor of the steerage compartment. Her body ached, but she couldn't be sure what had happened to her. She'd had nightmares as she slept... dreams about the nix and his deep-water palace of dead children, about the workhouse infirmary, about the smell of the ships with their damp decks and damaged hulls at Killala Bay. She dreamed of boys stealing stones from royal graves, and old men crawling to those same graves to return them. She wasn't sure what had happened to her or whether anything she remembered was real.

Margaret Sullivan borrowed a copy of Lola Montez's *The Arts of Beauty; Or, Secrets of a Lady's Toilet* from a woman in New Brunswick to read to Bridget in her cell.

> When Aristotle was asked why everybody was so fond of beauty, he replied, "It is the question of a blind man." Socrates described it as "a short-lived tyranny," and Theophrastus called it "a silent fraud."
> The Baroness de Stael confessed that she would exchange half her knowledge for personal charms, and there is not much doubt that most women of genius, to whom nature has denied the talismanic power of beauty, would consider it cheaply bought at that price.
> And let not man deride her sacrifice, and call it vanity, until he becomes himself so morally purified and intellectually elevated, that he would prefer the society of an ugly woman of genius to that of a great and match less beauty of less intellectual acquirements. All women know that it is beauty, rather than genius, which all generations of men have worshipped in our sex. Preach to the contrary as you may, there still stands the eternal fact, that the world has yet allowed no higher "mission" to woman, than to be beautiful.
>
> (xi)

Margaret watched Bridget's expression as she read. Bridget smiled sadly and touched the rough skin of her face thoughtlessly. Margaret, too, touched her skin, wondering for a moment if what the author, Lola Montez, had

Bridget's Hanging

written was true in any world—that a woman's highest mission was to be beautiful. Margaret had been taught that the great mission of any man or woman was to love God and offer loving service to others in patience and kindness. She was troubled reading such nonsense to an ill young woman who seemed to be so loosely tethered to reality, lying distended and pale on the bedding, staring up at the ceiling above her. She saw Bridget as a child playing princess with the foolish ideas planted in her infirm brain by the doctor's wife who had the money and the station to engage in such hedonism. But she was an unmindful child lost in the illusory universe of salons and drawing rooms.

Margaret was tempted to toss aside Montez's book and shake Bridget, to tell her to wake up and see that she was about be tried for murder, for her life, but she stopped herself out of kindness—out of heartbreak:

```
A history of all the arts which my sex have
employed, since her creation, to set off and
preserve her charms, would not only far exceed
the limits of this volume, but it would be a
tedious and useless book when written. I shall
confine myself mainly to the modern arts which
have fallen within my own observation during an
experience which has extended to nearly all the
courts and fashionable cities of the principle
nations of the earth.
```
(The Arts of Beauty, xii)

Bridget closed her eyes and remembered the night she spent in Liverpool before the *Orient* left port for New York City. She thought about how close she'd been to London, to the city where Lola Montez had spent so many days and nights charming the well-heeled, even spending an eventful evening in the Peeresses' or Women's Gallery for British nobility at the House of Lords. She imagined herself there, an important person, ennobled. She fell asleep that night thinking patrician thoughts.

Four

In June of 1866, the *Orient* arrived at the Port of New York City where as many as 169 or more immigrant ships also arrived that month. Between 1855 and 1891, newly arrived persons were ferried from their separate ports of entry to an arrival depot and processing station called Castle Garden in lower Manhattan. There, government officers tallied and recorded information such as country of origin, gender, age, religion, occupation, and value of everything brought into the United States. Because oceangoing vessels were often infested with rats, newly arrived citizens were compelled to bathe while their clothes and belongings were checked for rat and mice litters and hazardous animal waste. Immigrants who complained of illnesses or appeared ill were examined and most often treated by medical professionals, sometimes doctors and sometimes nurses. Most of the men and women who were ill were careful to appear healthy enough to be accepted as new citizens, as some with what were considered serious illnesses were "encouraged" to return to their countries of origin. With that in mind, Bridget Deignan insisted that her spells of dizziness and short bouts of spasms were the result of the ocean's rocking or motion sickness.

The compound known as Castle Garden on the island of Manhattan had been built between 1806 and 1808 to protect the area from British warships as Americans prepared for the inevitable War of 1812. The facility was originally called Fort Clinton, and it later became an élite society performance hall in which, interestingly, Lola Montez once danced her famous spider dance, an erotic version of a Spanish tarantella. Because of the size of and accommodations in the facility, the city eventually appropriated the compound and created an immigration center that provided protection from economic predators and unpredictable weather, provided some education about American practices and employment guidance, health services, and temporary shelter. Often, people seeking laborers or household assistance would go to Castle Garden and hire "hands," or employees. It was through this process that Bridget was hired by the Dayton family and traveled to New Jersey. Both Mr. Lewis Dayton and Mrs. Mary Dayton testified to this fact during Bridget's trial. Available records indicate that Lewis Dayton hired Bridget in July of 1866 as a domestic to assist his wife, Mary, in her house and with outdoor tasks on their farm.

Hiring domestics from Castle Garden was a common practice for many middle- and upper-class members of society in New York and New Jersey (Novatny). Records indicate that many businesses also regularly hired laborers from that location. According to Census documents, the Dayton family regularly traveled to Castle Garden to hire help as they owned a large home and sizeable piece of land for farming. Such records from 1870 further demonstrate that the Dayton family made it a general practice to hire domestic servants from Ireland. However, most of Castle Garden's records were destroyed in a fire 1897. But tracing and substantiating, when possible, all statements made in the media about or during the trial of Bridget Deignan is vital to understanding what actually occurred in 1867. This is especially important because a great deal of negative misinformation in the newspapers before Bridget's trial "helped" to convict her, as did contradictory testimony given during Bridget's grand jury and at her trial. Therefore, without objective and independently verified evidence, little newspaper reporting and nothing sworn to during these two assemblies is truly believable.

Such documents and research prove that Bridget did not work in New York City at any time as a prostitute or as a domestic servant, as Brendan claimed in his published "confession" and as some newspapers also claimed. Instead, she arrived in New York City and spent as many as three weeks at Castle Garden, during which time she received some education regarding the "exploitation" of immigrant workers, especially domestic servants, from the immigration workers trained to help new arrivals acclimate to their new country. Financial training, including currency equivalencies and salary guidelines, as well as some language instruction, was commonly offered. These facts are certain.

Bridget had always been a good listener; she didn't always understand what was being said, but she listened, and she tried to understand. She also remembered the things people said. She hung on the lessons given to her and the other recent arrivals at Castle Garden because she wanted so desperately to fit in into her new country. And in her imperfect way, she was determined to become an American and be Americanized, whatever that entailed. She noted how American women looked and dressed; this fact was obvious to anyone who followed her trial. Perhaps Bridget didn't look like an American, but the idea of what an American woman was and how she should behave had been planted in her head by Mrs. Coriell. Bridget saw herself as a kind of sister to American women, a sister to Mrs. Coriell, rather than a rival. She listened to the stories and magazine beauty lessons as Mrs. Coriell read them to her, and there was a girlish friendship between them.

Bridget was described at one point by a *New York Times* reporter as "an ordinary-looking Irish girl with plain features, that are not very expressive" (21 May 1867) and was also described by the same newspaper as "looking like fish after boiling" (30 April 1867). But these facts did not stop her from imagining herself as someone who could fit in to the middle-class world where she'd found herself working as a servant. This explains her behavior when visited in jail before, during, and after her trial. It would have been easy for her, in her limited understanding of the world, to imagine herself receiving callers as Mrs. Coriell had on Sunday afternoon after religious services.

Bridget's trial commenced on May 20, 1867. The night before her trial began, Mary Randolph and Margaret Sullivan attended Bridget in her cell

Bridget's Hanging

to pray with her in the hopes that God would direct the jury to find her not guilty. Mary and Margaret brought with them a modest dark beige suit for Bridget, and a pair of slightly used, brown boots because Bridget's feet and ankles were swollen from her relative inactivity in her cell. Mary also brought fresh undergarments she'd adjusted to better fit Bridget's distended frame. Bridget's underclothes had been bloody that night as they usually were, a symptom she'd long claimed was related to her falling disease. Although neither Mary nor Margaret had ever believed in that connection, they'd never questioned it directly. However, that night, as Bridget prepared herself to face the empaneled jury the next morning, she confessed a secret she'd tried to keep hidden from everyone in New Market and in Middlesex County.

Bridget told Mary and Margaret that after Mr. Dayton brought her from Castle Garden to New Jersey, she worked as a domestic for his family for two months. During that time, Bridget exhibited symptoms of her falling disease only once. It had been a minor fit, and she assured Mrs. Dayton that she did not need to see a doctor. She begged Mrs. Dayton to let it be, but Mrs. Dayton insisted. Bridget became very uncomfortable; she was afraid and left the Dayton household. She said that she was displeased with the wages she was being paid, and she quit (these facts was confirmed by Mr. Dayton's testimony in trial).

During the first days she was away from the Dayton household, she sought shelter at the railroad station in nearby New Brunswick. She went to the depot originally to find a train that would return her to Castle Garden. But when she arrived at the depot, she found it was a gathering spot for domestic servants and laborers who were without work, either temporarily or for the long term. It was a kind of haven for foreigners, misfits, and grifters. It was there that Bridget met Mary Gilroy.

Testimony of Mary Gilroy on May 26, 1867, as reported in the *New York Times*:

```
Mary Gilroy deposed as follows: I was born in
Ireland; am 43 years old; have been married
```

twice; the first time to Daniel Karr, who died in New-York about 15 years ago; the second time to Joe Gilroy, who was killed by the Sixth-avenue cars in New-York two years ago last Christmas; since that time have remained a widow; my own name was Mary McGinn; it is nearly 30 years since I first came to this country; first came to New York; came from New-York to New-Market since last Christmas; lived in New-Market two months; never saw Bridget Durgan until I saw her last Winter at Mr. Vails; while in New York I lived in a boarding-house. No. 49 Fourth-avenue.

26 May 1867

Mary Gilroy had been born Mary McGinn in Ireland sometime between 1818 and 1824. Her statements regarding her actual age changed from time to time. She had been in America for over thirty years and had lost most of her brogue, a fact that allowed her to fade into the background in polite society more than recent immigrants. Gilroy had survived a difficult childhood in Ireland and had been shipped to America by the pub owner who employed her mother. She'd worked as a charwoman at the Society of New York Hospital for almost four years, sleeping at night in the small living quarters there at the hospital. The pay was minimal at best, and the rations provided were meager, but the job provided shelter, a luxury that many immigrants were unable to find at that time.

During her time there, Gilroy found small ways to "enhance" her financial standing by taking items from the hospital and peddling them to shop owners and street vendors in the area. She maneuvered, conspired, and schemed her way into a better position at the hospital by offering small gifts to administrative nurses, and eventually became a nurse's assistant. She'd also developed a bit of savings she used to buy several stylish dresses she wore as she visited the shopkeepers who purchased the items she'd purloined from the hospital storage rooms. One man, Daniel Karr (sometimes spelled Kahar and Carr) was a street vendor or peddler who sold a variety of items from a pushcart. He dealt mostly in stolen goods but also sold candles that he made himself in his small basement room in a boardinghouse on Jay Street.

Mary McGinn married Karr, who schooled her in the art of confidence artistry. She continued to work at the Society of New York Hospital as a nurse's assistant until she was caught stealing a gold ring from a deceased patient. Hospital administrators retained her for arrest when they discovered that she'd hidden in her coat three flasks of laudanum, an opium derivative that her husband had been selling from his pushcart. But Mary had been well schooled by her husband, and she threatened the administrators with scandal by insisting she'd tell the police and anyone else who would listen about the doctors' errors she'd seen while working in the hospital. She said she'd call on the newspaper offices and tell them about the lack of cleanliness in the kitchens and the surgery rooms, the mice, and the patients who sometimes slept in their own excrement because of understaffing. And though the Society of New York Hospital was better than most hospitals operating in that era, the administration and the doctors feared the infamy a disgruntled employee could create if given the motive. She was released, and the police were never informed. The Karrs continued to make a living as street vendors, often unlawfully, for another year before Daniel Karr discovered the lucrative field of "resurrection."

"Resurrection men" were individuals who made a living stealing fresh corpses from tombs or graveyards and selling them to medical colleges and dissection schools. It had been a common practice in the United States and other nations to donate the bodies of executed criminals to medicals schools. This practice firmly entrenched the concept of medical dissection into the realm of the fire and brimstone of hell and eternal damnation. There were, however, not enough executions to supply the growing number of medical colleges and anatomy students with the necessary, not-yet-decayed corpses. So the often-unguarded graveyards of the poor and the potter's fields were easily harvested for bodies and for human teeth, which were also valuable for building dentures for wealthy individuals. For this reason, resurrectionists were as despised by the public as they were secretly required by anatomists and medical students.

Mary had maintained ties to a few of the other aides she'd met while working at the Society of New York Hospital and learned first about the value of human teeth taken from recently deceased patients. Later, she and Daniel learned about an outbuilding off Park Place near an expanding medical college where "night doctors" could deliver new corpses for a handsome fee, sometimes as much as twenty dollars each, depending on the level of decomposition. An array of potter's graveyards were always unguarded, many of which buried unclaimed bodies in multiple grave trenches. These seemed a relatively uncomplicated source of income for Daniel and Mary who used Daniel's cart to transport as many as three bodies at a time, depending on the size and weight of the corpse.

Daniel was a physically imposing man who learned quickly to pull sheathed bodies up through the loose soil with a minimum of digging. In only a matter of weeks, the two of them learned that Mary could attend burials as a former caregiver in order to determine the logistic placement of the bodies, the size, and sometimes the level of decomposition. Mary would sometimes claim dead bodies at poorhouses and asylums because, again, the donation of bodies to medical colleges was considered hellacious and immoral, a fate deserved only by the worst of convicted murderers.

In 1849, Daniel was arrested while digging up a fresh grave in a Catholic cemetery near Hallet's Cove in Queens. The body had been undisturbed, but Karr's intention was clear. Mary eluded police by hiding near a standing crypt on the northern end of the graveyard. Karr's pushcart was appropriated by police, who found the tools of the resurrectionist trade on it along with a collection of human teeth. The family's cold-water flat was searched; stolen jewelry and illegally obtained laudanum found.

Bridget's Hanging

Daniel was charged with larceny and sent to prison for eighteen months. Mary was forced to find another flat and a new source of income, and she spent most of 1850 in a 6th Ward shelter for women.

Mary then began assisting another resident, Mrs. El Thompson, who provided "women's services" in the basement of their residence. Mrs. Thompson advertised herself by word of mouth as "a doctor of all diseases related to irregularity and suppression or obstruction" of women's regular biology. Mary became the perfect assistant for "Dr. Thompson" as she had maintained many connections to her husband's criminal alliances as well as her sources of laudanum from her former place of employment. Together, the two women ran a successful abortion clinic.

Sheila Duane

Federal Census: see lines 25 & 36
https://familysearch.org
(Specific URLs subject to change)

Bridget's Hanging

Daniel Karr was released from prison in late 1851, suffering from tuberculosis; he later died at a charity hospital in Brooklyn.

Daniel Karr
> **Death Date:** 5 Jul 1852
> **Death Place:** New York City region, New York, United States
> The New York Genealogical and Biographical Record (quarterly 1832)—Extracts; Publication Place: *New York*; Publisher: *New York Genealogical and Biographical Society*.

In September 1854, Mary Karr met Joe Gilroy, a recent immigrant from Liverpool who'd been born and raised in Limerick, Ireland. Gilroy was very different from Mary's first husband. He was slight of build, gregarious, and hated labor of all kinds. He made his living as a pickpocket and as an expert in crimes of opportunity. Joe had neither the stomach nor the desire for the practices of the resurrectionist. He preferred to don his best duds and mix with gents in the courtyard of the Park Hotel or lunch at the curved mahogany bar where he'd find gullible wealthy men unused to protecting themselves from smooth confidence men. Joe also found success at the Metropolitan Hotel on Broadway and Prince Street, the Saint Nicholas Hotel on Broadway and Broome, and later the Fifth Avenue Hotel where well-heeled drinking men often lost track of a few dollars here or there. Though Joe could neither read nor write, he was always able to charm young women on the streetcars to relax their suspicions while he lifted their purses or to enchant the older British gents at the middle-class pubs whose wallets were often kept loosely in their jacket pockets.

Joe and Mary Gilroy were married in 1857, and they took residence in a flat off Jane Street in Greenwich Village. Joe was at that time being recognized in the finer establishments as a fellow who came around when money disappeared. He'd begun making his living exclusively on the streetcars, as a quick escape, when necessary, was possible. Mary continued working as an assistant nurse 'midwife,' a profession that had also become more difficult, as policing of crime and medical fraud became more sophisticated.

Just before Christmas 1864, Joe Gilroy was killed after he was caught pickpocketing a law clerk on the Sixth Avenue streetcar running on Canal Street. The clerk began struggling with Gilroy who had the man's wallet in his hand. Joe jumped from the streetcar and fell under a team of horses. He died at the scene.

Mary remained in New York City for approximately a year until Dr. Thompson was finally arrested and charged with the murder of six women who died because of botched medical abortions. Mary next hired herself out as a servant in New Jersey and eventually to the Vail family in New Market, New Jersey. It was then that Mary Gilroy met Bridget Deignan at the train station in New Brunswick, as that was the spot where Mary met other immigrant servants and laborers to share stories and libations.

Although it was clear to Mary Gilroy and her close friend, Annie Linen, that Bridget was neither a drinker nor a grifter, they took her under their wing both as an amusement and as a source of information about the Dayton family's financial dealings. Annie Linen and Mary Gilroy were both immigrants from Ireland, and both understood that Bridget was having difficulty acclimating herself to the United States. Annie, who was well acquainted with the fellows who worked at the depot, arranged for Bridget to stay in a temporary housing situation in a storage area attached to the railroad station. Bridget welcomed Annie's help and Mary's offer of biscuits and apples. Bridget stayed at the depot one night, and the next day confessed to Mary Gilroy that she was pregnant and had become pregnant because of an encounter she had while on the ship traveling to America. She confessed that, although she believed she remembered the encounter, it was not consensual nor could she be certain that what she remembered was what actually happened.

Although newspapers in 1867 printed much less information about Mary Gilroy's involvement in the murder of Mrs. Coriell, Mary Gilroy was also arrested after Mrs. Coriell's murder and was charged as an accessory.

Bridget's Hanging

Apparently, accessory cases were much less spectacular and sold fewer newspapers.

The Coriell Murder
Testimony Regarding the Alleged Complicity of Mary Gilroy.
From Our Own Correspondent,
New-Brunswick, N.J., Wednesday, June 5, 1867.

A mystery still surrounds the circumstances of the murderer of Mrs. CORIELL. No one seems to doubt the guilt of BRIDGET DURGAN, but whether or not she had an accomplice is still an open question. MARY GILROY, who is charged with having been accessory before the fact, is held in close confinement. The following is the important part of the evidence in her case taken by Justice NEVINS yesterday:

Samuel F. Randolph, jailor, testified that BRIDGET DURGAN told him that MARY GILROY was at Mrs. CORIELL's the night of the murder at about half-past six. Mrs. CORIELL was at supper; that Mrs. CORIELL did not see her as they were in the kitchen talking, and that Mary knew all about the murder; that a lamp placed in the back bedroom window upstairs was to be the signal, but she would not say what the signal was for; she also said that he, Mr. Randolph, and Dr. CORIELL knew the parties that were there that night, that they lived in Newmarket, and that she saw one of them in the Court-room during her trial; she then said that she, Bridget, was in the room all the time it was going on.

Delia Coyne fellow servant for the Vale family testified as follows: On the night of the murder I went to bed about half past nine; Mary went before me to bed; we slept in the same bed; Mary called me when she heard the cry of fire; she was sitting up by the window when she called me; she asked me to come and raise the window, as she didn't understand raising the window; I went and raised it, but Mary had often raised the window before in the morning; while we were at the window, Mary said, "I think that Bridget has murdered Mrs. Coriell;" at that time it was not known that Mrs. Coriell was murdered; Mary said when she first got up, there was no noise; that she had walked the room a long time; that she had cramps very bad and was afraid to get in bed; that she heard Mrs. Coriell say, "Spare my life," &c., and that she thought she heard Bridget's voice; that the noise rose to such an extent that she got into bed and covered her head with the bedclothes; I was asleep and did not hear anything of the noise until Mary called me; Mrs. Vale told me the next morning that Ms. Coriell was killed.

Miss Cynthia F. Onderdonk deposed that a day or two after Mary Gilroy was brought to the jail at New-Brunswick, she went there to ascertain from her the whereabouts of Delia Coyne, as she wished to employ her as a servant; she went into the kitchen, and after she had obtained the information, the conversation turned upon the subject of the murder. Mary said that Mrs. Coriell had not died a day too soon; that Mrs. Coriell had insulted her when she came over to the house for medicine; I asked how she came to insult her; she said she went to the Doctor's and Mrs. Coriell asked her if she was the woman that had the asthma and came so often for medicine; she said she was, and then Mrs. Coriell said she guessed she didn't come for medicine, but came to see the doctor, and that insult she said she couldn't overlook, that she had never liked her since then; I was at Mr. Vail's, Newmarket, and dined there the day Mrs. Coriell was buried; they told me there that Mary had heard the noise, and when I came to the jail I asked her if she heard the screaming that night over to the Doctor's; she replied that she did hear it, but thought it was the noise of a drunken woman that was walking up and down the road; I said, "It's a pity you had not known it was murder, so that you could have given the alarm and saved her;" she said, "Not a hand would I have raised if I had known it;" Mary also said that if Dr. Coriell got another wife she hoped he would get one that was worthy of him and had a little common sense.

While these witnesses were testifying, Mary Gilroy frequently interrupted them, telling the Justice to "stop their lies." The Justice called her to order several times.

NYT 6 June 1867

Bridget continued to tell her story to Margaret Sullivan and Mary Randolph on the night before her trial began. They listened to Bridget with both distress and a kind of numbness. Both Margaret and Mary knew that Mary Gilroy had been arrested as an accessory to the murder of Mrs. Coriell, and that Mary Gilroy was a well-known undesirable who remained in the community only by virtue of her capacity for labor and her skill as a kitchen maid. In fact, Mary Gilroy was in that jail at that moment locked in the row of cells on the second floor just above the women as they listened to Bridget's confusing and miserable story.

Bridget continued the tale, saying Mary Gilroy brought her to be examined by her doctor friend, Dr. William Coriell, whom she'd once seen and who also lived in New Market. Bridget had met him once at the Daytons' home. Dr. Coriell had a small office on the first floor of his house where Bridget eventually became a domestic servant. He examined her, confirmed that she was pregnant, and spoke to Mary Gilroy for some time in a hushed voice.

Mary Gilroy asked Bridget if she had any money she could pay to have her encumbrance removed. Bridget said she'd been given some money before she left the Dayton household and that the family owed her two dollars more. Bridget told this part of her story to Mary Randolph and Margaret Sullivan as she cried softly and tried in her often inarticulate brogue to explain why she could say nothing about the identity of Mrs. Coriell's killers. Mary Gilroy and the two men who'd beaten and stabbed Mrs. Coriell knew about the child, knew about her sin. If her priest ever discovered it, she'd be condemned to hell. Bridget was adamant. She said that no one else knew this secret—her pregnancy and its ending—except Mary Gilroy and the people Mary had told who used the secret to manipulate and frighten her. Bridget told them that Dr. Coriell, too, knew about her pregnancy, and knew Mary Gilroy performed the procedure that terminated it.

Neither Mary Randolph nor Margaret Sullivan could really understand this logic that had forced Bridget to keep silent about the murderers. The two women knew that the Lord knew about the pregnancy…the

Bridget's Hanging

Lord knew that child's life had been ended. Wasn't it the Lord who would condemn or forgive Bridget? And if she confessed to her priest, didn't her religion state that her priest could offer her the Lord's forgiveness if indeed she was truly sorry? Was Bridget's flawed belief an outgrowth of her Romanism or her infantile inability to grasp the real meaning of her own faith? Would explaining this fallacy to Bridget bring any positive results?

For a moment the three women were silent. In the distance were the muffled sounds of a man's voice and the clicking of boots on the wooden floor above. Then Bridget's expression changed, and she began to retell the story of her father's childhood outing to Queen Maeve's cairn and the curse that had befallen her family. She wondered aloud whether he'd ever managed to keep his promise and return a stone to that haunted grave. Then, as if in an epiphany, she looked frightened and asked whether Queen Maeve would amplify her curse if she discovered that the stone returned by her father was not the original stone but a ruse, a hoax to deceive the queen into lifting her curse. Bridget became visibly shaken, and her breathing became shallow. Her eyes were wide and filled with panic. "What can be done now?" she asked. "Is it too late for me now?"

Through the small jail window came the sounds of a railroad train moving west toward Pennsylvania. The sound reminded Bridget of the laments of keening women she'd heard while growing up, the piercing—often breathless—rhymed chants and moans of mourning women at the graves of loved ones, of the worthy, the brave. Though the train moved away from the jail, the lamenting seemed to be moving closer to Bridget as she imagined herself walking the steps up to the gallows.

She remembered one "bean ag caoineadh" or a keening woman called Brona who wept at all the open graves when Bridget was very young in Sligo. She would cry, pray, and call to the man in the grave to get up, to come up from the moist ground, and go home. At the grave of her mother's brother, Lee, who died of exposure after working the port in Keel, Mayo, Brona cursed the Keel Strand and the cold winds that ushered in the banshee as keeners often did. Brona cursed the Keel Strand that killed him with labor, the winds that killed him with cold, and the crown for ruining the souls of Hibernia. The keener called Lee to come up from his grave and sleep that night in his own bed. For Bridget, the only keening would be the steel screech and steam trumpet of that lumbering train creeping toward the Delaware River to the west.

Five

> "She asked me if I knew how to write; I said I did; she said she wanted to write three or four lines to the Doctor; I told her it was not necessary to write to the Doctor, because she could speak to him; she said she knew that, but she had done so before."
>
> Testimony of Asa Bush as reported in the
> *NYT* 21 May 1867

The first mention of Bridget Deignan's trial in the *New York Times* was in the issue dated 30 April 1867, approximately two months after the murder. The *New York Times* reporter offered a general, albeit biased, review of the events of February 25–26 and what followed.

> On the morning of the 26th of February last, BRIDGET DURGAN, a servant girl living in the family of Dr. CORIELL at New-Market, N.J., went to one of the neighbors carrying one of the children in her arms, and stated that two men had broken into the house and murdered her mistress. The residents of the little country village gathered at once at the house, and found

the tale true to the extent that the murder had been done. Dr. CORIELL had been absent from home the previous night and had not yet returned, and there were no signs of any forcible entry having been made into the house. The contradictory statements of the girl BRIDGET fastened suspicion upon her as the real murderess of MARY ELLEN CORIELL, and she was taken into custody. Since then, the District-Attorney has been diligently engaged in working up the case, and had found sufficient evidence to establish a prima facie case against the accused, who was accordingly last week indicted by the Grand Jury, and yesterday the case was called before the Middlesex County Oyer and Terminer, at the Court-house in New-Brunswick, N.J.

The prisoner has little of the appearance popularly connected with that of a murderess. She is an Irish woman, apparently about thirty years of age, of medium height, full habit, and a moon face of ruddy hue and heavy under jaw. Her only really forbidding feature is the eye, and even that is more an index of stupidity than malice, having the appearance so well likened to that of fish after boiling. She came into Court walking briskly, and even gaily, with a smile upon her countenance, and during the morning sat an apparently uninterested spectator of the proceedings.

As soon as the prisoner was seated her counsel rose and moved a continuance of the cause. The reasons alleged in favor of the motion were that sufficient time had not been allowed for the preparation of the defense, the prisoner having been arraigned upon the indictment only one week ago. The counsel alleged that he had diligently employed the time in endeavors to be ready for trial at this date, but owing to the fact that he had been unable to find the witnesses for the defense had failed.

It appeared from the statements of her counsel that the prisoner is totally without means; in his own words, "She has not a dollar in the world," which is sufficiently evidenced by the fact that her counsel is assigned her by the Court, and receive their compensation from the State.

30 April 1867

On Monday, May 20, 1867, the trial of Bridget Deignan began. Bridget was charged with the February 25, 1867, murder of Mrs. Mary Ellen Coriell, her mistress and employer. People across the country who could read a newspaper or listen to a conversation knew as soon as the trial began what the outcome would be. In fact, many newspapers had published Bridget's "confession" as early as the beginning of March, just days after the murder, even though nothing Bridget said could really be understood as a confession. "Bridget Durgan, the servant girl, has confessed in the murder of Mrs. Dr. Coriell at Newmarket, New Jersey" (*Boston Journal* 7 March, *Boston Traveler* 7 March, *Daily National Intelligencer* 15 March, *Evening Star* 29 March, *Clearfield Republican* 21 March 1867, etc.). On March 1, 1867, the *Richmond Dispatch* ended its article about the murder with the following: "What provocation the murderess had to commit the deed is as yet but a matter of conjecture."

From the beginning, the prosecutor in Bridget's trial, Mr. Charles Herbert, portrayed Bridget as subhuman and animalistic. Bridget was indicted for four counts of "inflicting with a butcher knife a mortal wound on the left side of the neck, and with inflicting wounds on the head, face, neck, breast, stomach, and other parts of the body of the murdered woman with some sharp instrument unknown," according to written records. Mr. Herbert described the victim, Mary Ellen Coriell, calling her a lovely woman, "adorned with all the virtues of a wife and mother," and stressed that she had been butchered in her own home by a soulless immigrant fiend who sat before the jury on that very day. Newspapers reported and printed his every eloquent word.

Researchers in the history of execution in the United States and abroad have linked the psychology behind death penalty to not only nativist superiority, but to the "legal" and media portrayal of defendants as subhuman or animalistic. In his book *"The Penalty Is Death": U.S. Newspaper Coverage of Women's Executions*, Marlin Shipman, professor of journalism, reviews the media coverage of Mary Ellen Coriell's murder and the charges against Bridget, her trial, and execution. He states, "Killing a human being is more acceptable if the person killed is perceived as less than human. This is true with war or capital punishment. If the public perceives a condemned inmate as more animal than human, then executions are made more palatable" (171).

The prosecutor and the press consistently referred to Bridget as a fiend and compared her to Mrs. Coriell, who fit perfectly into the 1867 concept of a classic and ideal American woman. Without using the word *immigrant*, Herbert played on the nativist, anti-Catholic prejudices of the men in the jury. And the subtext of his statement regarding Mrs. Coriell's "loveliness" ("a woman of uncommon beauty and suavity of manners") was Bridget's unattractiveness ("looking like fish after boiling," as reported by the press) brought about both by her illness and her inactivity during her time in a jail cell.

Further, Shipman's text asserts the presence of the press in the minds of the jury. "The press plays an important role in this process because most of what the public knows about a condemned defendant, it learns through press reports. How the press 'labels' and describes defendants probably are important, especially before trial. Some researchers contend that most people believe that press descriptions of defendants are real and accurate" (171). The local press had labeled Bridget as "a cunning evil doer" dominated by her own "moral ugliness" (*New York Herald* 27 February 1867) just after the murder.

The *New York Herald* was a daily newspaper very familiar in the New Brunswick/New Market area, and it was at the time the most profitable and—in most cases—the most popular newspaper in the United States. On February 27, the headline of the article describing the murder of Mrs. Coriell was, "MURDER AT NEWMARKET, N.J." while the subheading read, "A Lady Literally Butchered by Her Servant Girl." There were many such "verdicts" made by the press before Bridget's trial even began. Shipman maintains, "By the mid-1800s, Irish Catholics emigrated mainly to the United States, and they became easy targets for American nativist and anti-Catholic prejudice" (172). And this was the atmosphere that informed the press and Bridget's jury in 1867. It's no wonder that reporters from the *New York Times* consistently wrote about certain conviction.

The judge presiding over the trial was Judge Peter Vrendenburgh of Freehold, a member of a wealthy, landholding Dutch family. The attorney general at the time was George Robeson, who later, after the accolades of Bridget's conviction, became a member of President Grant's cabinet. The district attorney was Mr. Charles Herbert, an attorney who practiced in Middlesex County and often appeared before Judge Vrendenburgh. Bridget's court-appointed defense team consisted of Garnett Adrian, son of a prominent nineteenth-century mathematician, who most often served as a public defender, and William Leupp, former mayor of New Brunswick, also a public defender.

Mr. Herbert began his prosecution by reviewing the details of the murder of Mrs. Coriell. On the morning of February 25, at the home Dr. William Coriell shared with his wife and daughter, a fire, limited to a single room, was extinguished and the body of Mrs. Coriell was discovered. Herbert stated that Mrs. Coriell was stabbed to death with a knife owned by her own family, though he admits that he couldn't prove beyond a reasonable doubt that the family's knife was the murder weapon. Herbert told the entirely male, white jury that "this was no common case of homicide that they were about to investigate. A lovely woman, adorned with all the virtues of a wife and mother, in her own home is butchered by a fiend" (*NYT* 21 May 1867). Herbert went on, "Dr. Coriell had left his house at four o'clock in the afternoon and returned to find his wife murdered and his child motherless" (5/21).

Herbert called Dr. William Coriell, the husband of the murder victim, to the stand during the first day's testimony. Dr. Coriell recounted his circumstances before his wife's murder. He shared his home with his wife, Mary Ellen; his daughter, Mary, who was often called Mamey; Asa Bush, his yardman; and Bridget Durgan, who'd lived with his family since October 22, 1866. Dr. Coriell testified that he and his wife planned to discharge Bridget at the end of the month. He stated that Bridget "offered to stay for a dollar or two less; she did not want to leave" (*NYT* 5/21). He further testified that Bridget "has always shown a peaceable disposition," and that he and his wife always trusted her with their child and running the operations of their home. "Mrs. Coriell and I had perfect confidence in Bridget up to this occurrence; we thought Bridget an honest woman; we frequently left her in charge of the house, sometimes with the child when we went out; she seemed fond of my child and the child usually fond of her" (*NYT* 5/21).

Dr. Coriell stated, "Bridget was taken sick the Tuesday previous to the murder, and continued so till Friday; she had catalepsy, arising from a

Bridget's Hanging

female disorder, which was removed and she recovered entirely; a spot of blood from such a cause might possibly fasten itself upon a skirt or other article of clothing in case of contact" (5/21). Bridget's defense team would later use this fact to explain the single spot of blood on her skirt near her thigh the morning after the murder described by witnesses. Her defense also stressed that no other blood spots were found anywhere on Bridget's person or clothing.

Coriell's testimony continued, "I told her she might stay a few days until fully recovered; such fits so caused leave no permanent effects after the patient is restored; catalepsy and epilepsy are similar but are always distinguishable; catalepsy and epilepsy may alternate but not usually; catalepsy may sometimes lead to idiocy; in her previous sickness when I visited her, she had the same difficulty...Bridget's fit produced loss of muscular power and consciousness; it was not hysterical" (*NYT* 5/21). Dr. Coriell's testimony asserted that Bridget had never demonstrated any aggressive behavior or ill will toward his family. It also demonstrated that Bridget was physically ill; he'd initially met her when he was called to give her medical treatment while she worked for the Dayton family.

Asa Bush, the Coriell's yardman and farrier, took the stand the same day. He stated that Bridget had spoken to him in the barn the day Mrs. Coriell was murdered. Bush testified that Dr. Coriell told him "to stay around a while after dark; I then milked and did my chores; while I was busy in the barn Bridget came with a basket of cobs; I tilled it and gave it to her; she asked me if I knew how to write; I said I did; she said she wanted to write three or four lines to the Doctor; I told her it was not necessary to write to the Doctor, because she could speak to him; she said she knew that, but she had done so before; she then went into the house...all was harmonious in Dr. Coriell's household" (*NYT* 5/22).

Bridget's defense team would later use this testimony as the confirmation of her innocence, stating that she was fearfully aware that a person or persons planned to enter the Coriell home that night and rob the family.

Either she'd been unintelligible in her attempt to warn Dr. Coriell, or he'd misunderstood her because of her brogue. Bush's undisputed testimony demonstrated that Bridget had both spoken to Dr. Coriell in an attempt to warn him about the upcoming robbery and had attempted to have him warned by letter through Asa Bush.

The timing of the planned robbery, the defense suggested, was important for Bridget's vindication because she was about to leave the Coriell family to find new employment elsewhere. The robbers wanted Bridget's assistance, so they had to act before she left the household. Further, Mary Gilroy had been jailed in the same facility wherein Bridget was confined since her arrest for conspiracy to the murder of Mrs. Coriell. Although Bridget had not implicated her immediately after the murder, she'd confided Mary Gilroy's participation to Mr. Randolph privately. Hearsay evidence, that is, statements made by Mary Gilroy to several members of the community, had convinced law enforcement that Mary was a party to or the mastermind behind the robbery that became a murder. And, though never suggested by the defense, Mary may have "blackmailed" Bridget, using the fact of her abortion as the inducement for her cooperation. Mary Gilroy had, in fact, "removed" the encumbrance that had created Bridget's catalepsy. Mary, it seems, had threatened Bridget with hell. "Wide is the gate that opens to hell" was a common translation of Matthew 7:13–14 among the Irish.

The majority of testimony against Bridget was unscientific and clearly biased. The most damning evidence, according to members of the community, was what appeared to be a bite mark on Mrs. Coriell's face, which was noted after her death. Rev. Charles Little, a neighbor of the Coriell family, who'd taken it upon himself to "charge" Bridget with the murder, testified as follows:

```
I saw marks of teeth on the corpse about 10
o'clock that day. They were on the right side of
the face and a little way in front and below the
```

```
ear; there were four print-marks of peculiar
arrangement; the impress was in a semi-circle;
two of them were apparently regular and the two
others were pointing outward I had a conver-
sation with Bridget on the day of the inquest
when it was proposed to take the imprint of her
teeth; some wax was prepared, and I told her
to make an impression lightly with her teeth on
the wax; she made an impression about three-
fourths of an inch deep; she bit through the
wax; I asked her again two or three times to
make it lightly; I did not succeed in getting
the impression we wanted.
```
NYT 22 May 1867

The supposed "bite mark" evidence was questionable then and is still considered unreliable in 2016 (Mawajdeh). Reverend Little, a neighbor of the Coriell family with no medical or police training, made the wax impression of Bridget's teeth because, he champions, he just knew she had committed the crime. He also testified that he forced Bridget to repeatedly bite the wax block because he wasn't getting the impression that he "wanted." The other witnesses against her expressed their clear prejudice against her. For example, members of the Little family refused to open the door to Bridget after the murder because Reverend Little thought she was asking for help for "some Irish family" called Curry. Both Mrs. Little and her son testified that they knew Bridget had murdered Mrs. Coriell, even though all the witnesses also testified that Bridget was a quiet young woman who behaved virtuously and properly at all times before the murder. In fact, witnesses for the prosecution insisted that Bridget had always behaved in a civil, quiet, and peaceable manner. Somehow, though, she had become, for a brief time, a murderer and a fiend.

Also used as evidence against Bridget were four small cuts on her left hand (she was right-handed) that she'd gotten while washing clothes with pins left in them. She also had a spot of blood on the back of her underskirt where menstrual or blood from hemorrhaging would attach. As stated, Dr. Coriell in his testimony admitted that Bridget's health problems were related to her menstrual cycle and caused bleeding. Bridget also had a very small cut on her upper lip. The other testimony against her was rooted in conversations she'd had with members of the community after the murder. People had felt compelled to accuse her, and her responses were often unclear or clouded by her Hibernian brogue, a fact that was repeatedly admitted on the witness stand.

Although reporters often commented on Bridget's apparent disinterest in the trial, her history suggests that she wasn't able to fully grasp the vocabulary of the lawyers participating in her defense and prosecution. "Beyond a little nervousness during the reading of the indictment and the District-Attorney's address, there was nothing in her demeanor to indicate how deeply she was interested in the proceedings" (*NYT* 21 May 1867). Statements such as these peppered the news reports of the trial, but Bridget's preoccupation with what she believed was the curse of Queen Maeve and magic clews and banshees crowded her unsophisticated mind to the point that her actual circumstances may have seemed vague and unimportant. For instance, as Bridget remembered cutting her hands on the pins left in clothes as she washed them...she probably recalled one of the versions of the banshee legend that contends banshees sometimes appear as laundresses who rinse blood from the clothing of the people whose deaths they have come to portend.

In the workhouse infirmary, there was so much laundering of bloody clothes and washing of blood-stained hands that Bridget believed banshees were ever-present there, always prognosticating the death of a child or a mother or brother. Perhaps she even began to believe that she, with her constant hemorrhage, had become a banshee and was forewarning the death of someone close to her, or her own death. She was like a child with childish fears and imaginings.

On the morning after Mary Ellen Coriell was murdered, Bridget repeated the story about robbers to Dr. Coriell and the other residents of New Market who interrogated her. She stated that two men appeared at the Coriell home about seven thirty, looking for the doctor. She said they did not at that time state their business. Mrs. Coriell told them that her husband had gone to Piscataway, New Jersey, and was attending to a woman in labor. The two men stated that they would go to Piscataway and speak to the doctor directly. Bridget then said the two men returned about ten thirty and knocked at the kitchen door. Bridget opened the door, believing the doctor had returned home. When Mrs. Coriell saw the two men, she became frightened either because of the late hour or because she was afraid the men had negative intentions. Mrs. Coriell, according to Bridget, called out to her to go and get Dr. Coriell, so Bridget took the baby and ran to seek help.

When she was asked to identify the two men, Bridget identified Barney Doyle and Michael Hunt, both employed either by the railroad or by the railroad depot. The railroad depot at that time was a gathering center for laborers between jobs, domestic servants, and people who were not welcome in the middle-class areas of New Jersey society. There were people who lived at the depot as caretakers, including John Keagan, Margaret Keagan, and Anne Quigley. Quigley and Mary Gilroy were friends who often made extra money selling trinkets they'd "found" and medications that Mary came across here and there with the help of her friends at the Society of New York Hospital. The depot was a sanctuary for gamblers, misfits, and grifters. The disenfranchised of New Jersey found it a safe place to talk about fraud, robbery, and revenge. And for most of the people there, that talk was just that—empty thoughts and talk.

Barney Doyle had a reason to dislike Dr. Coriell; his son had died after Dr. Coriell treated him for some illness. His wife, Catherine Doyle, may have given the child too much medication, which caused an overdose and death...Dr. Coriell may have failed to adequately treat his child...or the child's death may have just been an unavoidable tragedy. Michael Hunt lived with the Doyle family and may have been affected by the tragic death of the child, so he, too, may have disliked Dr. Coriell.

Anne Linen, an eighteen-year-old servant girl in the community, who was also accused by Bridget within hours of Mrs. Coriell's murder, was Michael Hunt's girlfriend. It's clear from the alibi testimony given on behalf of Doyle, Hunt, and Linen that they were regular visitors to the depot and probably participated in the rebellious talk that often occurred there. Circumstantial evidence suggests that Doyle and Hunt talked about robbing the Coriell house and wanted to do so before Bridget left to find work elsewhere. This may have been why Bridget tried to warn the doctor on her last night in his home.

Bridget also claimed that the two men involved, Doyle and Hunt, had forced her to swear on a Bible that she would never relate anything that they or anyone who participated in the illicit, private discussions at the railroad depot said or did.

```
Dr. Coriell said: "Well Bridget, you've sent
for me to come down here. What have you to say?
She said that Barney Doyle and another man came
to Dr. Coriell's house several times; one night
they took her out on the walk and made her take
three oaths and kiss the Bible, that she would
never tell anything that might happen hereaf-
ter; she told this over and over, and he said if
you have anything to tell me, say it; she asked
the doctor if he did not think she would see him
again. He told her she would not; it was only
that she had sent for him that he had come then;
```

after the doctor went out of the cell, after a while she sent for him again; she then asked him if he did not remember a certain night that someone came after him from Brooklyn; he said he did remember some one coming from Brooklyn or Samptown; she asked if he did not remember telling the man to walk on and he would overtake him; he said he did; she asked if he didn't remember coming into the kitchen and seeing her stand in the kitchen door talking to some man standing outside; he said he did; she said 'that man was going to follow you that night, but was afraid he could not overtake you before you overtook the man, so he did not go; the doctor asked if she had any more to say; she said, "If Asa had written that letter, as I wanted him to, the thing would not have happened;" the Doctor asked what letter; she said she wanted Asa to write a few lines to send him; the Doctor asked what she wanted to write; she said she wanted to write for him to come home; that she was afraid something would happen while he was away; he asked if she knew anything was going to happen before he left home; if she did she ought to have told him; she said she did not know it was going to happen, but was afraid it would.

NYT 24 May 1867

It seems that Doyle, Hunt, Gilroy, and perhaps Anne Linen had discussed robbing the Coriells on that last night Bridget was in their employ. The two men probably called at the house about 7:30 that evening; that fact was not disproved by trial testimony. And it is known that Mary Gilroy had a motive to both rob and kill Mrs. Coriell and was, in all probability, party to the discussions about robbing the Coriell home. She had a strong reason to dislike Mrs. Coriell for insulting her. "Mrs. Coriell had insulted her when she came over to the house for medicine…and that insult she said she couldn't overlook" (*NYT* 6 June 1867).

Mary Gilroy had a criminal past and behaved in a suspicious manner after Mrs. Coriell's murder. Further evidence of her guilt, according to the district attorney, was a statement she'd made after the murder: "Not a hand would I have raised if I had known it," Mary claimed after the murder, further stating, that "if Dr. Coriell got another wife she hoped he would get one that was worthy of him and had a little common sense" (*NYT* 6 June 1867). Though the suggestion that Mary Gilroy was the murderer or at least involved is based on circumstantial evidence, this circumstantial evidence is more compelling than the hearsay testimony against a woman too ill to leave her place of employment and who had always been a trusted and well-mannered employee.

Mary Gilroy's trial was scheduled to begin in September, just after the scheduled execution of Bridget. On August 14, the *New York Tribune* reported on the disposition of the case against Mary Gilroy who was jailed in a cell just above Bridget's cell. She'd been jailed almost as long as Bridget had and spoken often to newspaper reporters. "She greets all with a smile who visit her, and is ever willing to engage in conversation. Her looks very strongly exhibit the effect of her comparatively short confinement. She has a nervous excitable temperament, and in conversation with her one has to be very guarded or her anger will rise, and then conversation must cease instantly." According to reporters, Mary was always quick to criticize Bridget for naming her as the murderer, and insisted that any implication of her guilt was false. According to the *New York Tribune* reporter, Mary stated, "Bridget has made a number of confessions to a number of persons, and there is no truth in any of them" (8/14).

Bridget's Hanging

It's also important to note that Bridget was still being influenced, perhaps even threatened, by Mary Gilroy while in jail. Mary's cell was directly above Bridget's and Mary would often drop items that would land directly in front of Bridget's cell. One *New York Times* reporter wrote, "I now left the cell and was informed by the jailer, Mr. RANDOLPH, that while I had been talking with BRIDGET, MARY GILROY, who is confined in the jail, but has been allowed to walk about outside of her cell, had stood on the balcony of the second story above and opposite to BRIDGETS'S cell, and dropped a ball of yarn down" (*NYT* 3 June 1867). Seemingly harmless in itself, the ball of yarn, a clew in fact, was probably the most hostile reminder for Bridget of the power Mary Gilroy had over her ultimate fate.

In June of 1867, Bridget may not yet have resigned herself to her fate on the gallows, but she must have resigned herself to the fact that she could never publicly admit Mary Gilroy's guilt or at least complicity in the murder. Bridget was a very simple and superstitious girl who'd lived in rural Ireland, a place dominated at that time by starvation and magical thinking. The ball of yarn Mary Gilroy dropped served as a reminder of her father's stories about the magic clew and the Isle of the Blest, the clew that pulled travelers back to the place of promises…but also a place of captivity. In the Irish story, the "Voyage of Bram," Bram was invited to the Otherworld where he planned to live a thousand years without troubles. But Bram and his men discovered that the enchanted Isle of Women among the islands of the Otherworld was like a prison from which they couldn't escape. As the travelers tried to embark and free themselves, they were pulled back by a mythical, powerful clew or ball of thread. They couldn't leave without being lost forever.

Bridget may have once believed that her father was right—that returning that stone to Queen Maeve's grave would lift the curse on his family; that the clew she would find would lead her to an enchanted life in a new land where memories of the old world would die; and that she would find in America a kind of heaven just like the travelers did in the imramha or stories her father told her when she was a girl. But it was becoming increasingly difficult for her to believe such things as her trial moved toward its conclusion.

On May 30, the second chair of Bridget's defense team, Mr. William Leupp, began his closing statement by outlining the element of time as it affected the evidence on the night of the murder. He insisted that the case against his client was circumstantial and included no positive evidence. Bridget's was a case of bigotry alone, fed into by the biased reporting of the press. He emphatically stated, "But the spring of prejudice had welled up till the torrent swept all New Market with it" (*NYT* 5/30). Leupp insisted that his client had neither the disposition nor the physical strength to murder another adult. "She was a weak, uncultivated girl—an innocent, taciturn, retiring, modest girl" (*NYT* 5/30).

> Mr. Leupp read over the testimony of the witness referred to, in which is detailed the story of the accused concerning the coming of two men to Dr. Coriell's house. Those two men came to rob the house, and he was sorry to say that he believed that Bridget knew that they were to come, but that she had nothing to do with the murder.
> Those two men committed the murder, and he was astonished that the prosecution had not perceived it and ceased from their idolatry of a false theory and bowed to the truth. Bridget had heard, no matter how, that the attack was to be made that night. She had asked Asa Bush to write to Dr. Coriell for her, and if he had done it the tragedy would not have taken place

He spoke severely of the zealous efforts of the detectives to fasten the crime on the defendant. Their effort was not to ascertain who did the deed, but it was their foregone conclusion that she did the deed, and every inquiry of theirs was directed at proving that.

He next examined the effort of the prosecution to prove that there was the imprint of teeth on Mrs. Coriell's neck. Unless it was shown that these marks were the marks of teeth, the evidence went for nothing. No witness said that the marks were certainly the marks of teeth. Some witnesses thought they were, and one referred to them as possibly having been made by a poker. That was the theory of that witness. Dr. Decker said there were some scratches made by nails, and that was the way in which these marks were made. The truth was staring them in the face that these were the marks of nails, but this miserable prosecution, and the witnesses wedded to its theory, could not, for a moment, see it.

And now what was the result of the searching review of the evidence that had been made? Was not the charge against the defendant swept away? Had it not been for the prejudice in which the case was saturated the accusation would not have come to Court with any degree of credibility.

It was in evidence that Bridget had said that she had been forced some time before, by some men, to take an oath on the Bible, and kiss the book, that she never would disclose what she knew if anything should afterward happen to the Coriells. She had a religious sentiment. That oath she deemed binding. She was afraid to speak of it, but if Asa Bush had written, as she wanted him to do, to Dr. Coriell, the tragedy would have been prevented.

   At the close of the session the prisoner appeared to be seized with a fit, which lasted for a few minutes only.

NYT 30 May 1867

On May 31, the attorney general, George M. Robeson, offered his closing statement in the case against Bridget. A closing statement by an attorney general in such as case was at that time very unusual, but Bridget's case had become a media sensation. People in every state were reading about the 'Roman illiterate immigrant' who'd murdered her American mistress. It seems that Bridget had begun to understand that her fate had been sealed. She'd managed to maintain her composure through most days during the trial, but on that day, she began to cry as Robeson recounted the events of the day and evening that Mrs. Coriell was killed. Robeson stressed repeatedly that the prosecution had not been biased against the defendant. He acknowledged that the case against Bridget was circumstantial, but insisted that "the degree of circumstantiality" (*NYT* 31 May 1867) demanded that Bridget be condemned to hang. Robeson recalled the defendant's changing stories and the testimony of people who offered their own opinions about what might have happened—what could have happened the night of the murder. Then Robeson offered his own scenario as to what may have happened:

He developed the theory that one or more persons went upstairs to the bureau, and perhaps upset it, and Mrs. Coriell, who had partly undressed and laid down, heard the noise, arose, slipped on an old dress, started to go upstairs, met the murderers or murderesses, fled before them to her bedroom, was followed by them, one of them with a tablecloth in her hand from the bureau upstairs which is dropped in the bedroom, and the murder was committed, and there ensued the second final struggle as before detailed

    He expressed surprise that counsel for the defense had admitted that Bridget knew that a burglary was to be committed. Did he not know that a servant who admitted a burglar to rob and murder was guilty as a principal, and guilty of murder in the first degree. The fact that the defendant was a woman gave every reason for the long, careful, favoring investigation of her case; but when it was found that she had unsexed herself and committed such a monstrous crime she could claim no sympathy.

NYT 31 May 1867

When Robeson was finished, the spectators in the courtroom applauded.

At that time, Judge Vrendenburgh instructed the jury. He stated unequivocally that if Bridget assisted the murderers in any way, even if she had not participated in the murder, she was guilty of murder. If Bridget was present, she was guilty of murder. The judge asked the jury, "Was there evidence that she was wicked enough to do it?" (*NYT* 31 May 1867). The judge reminded the jury that evidence suggested Bridget had been aware of the plot against the Coriells, even asking Asa Bush to write a note of warning. The judge further stressed the importance of the bite mark evidence: "If these were her teeth was it not as strong proof that she murdered Mrs. Coriell as if she had impressed her photograph on Mrs. Coriell or pinned a paper to the body on which were the words, 'I did it,' signed by her?" (*NYT* 31 May 1867). Vrendenburgh's language to the jury proved he himself had spent fifteen years as prosecutor of the pleas.

Vrendenburgh insisted to the jury that the evidence pointed to the guilt of Bridget Deignan and stated that cruelty could have indeed been the only motive for the murder.

> The judge entered into a detailed description of the wounds as given by the witnesses. "Who," he asked, "did this midnight deed of horror?" Was the defendant present? The weight to be given to circumstantial evidence depended upon the cogency of the circumstances. Where circumstances existed, it was as safe to convict on circumstantial as on direct evidence. Positive witnesses might be mistaken or deceived, but circumstances might spring from a thousand things and point shortly to the perpetrators of crime. Now, did the circumstances prove that the defendant participated in the crime? She had the opportunity to do it. Was there evidence that she was wicked enough to do it? The judge recalled the evidence that Bridget was cognizant of the conspiracy to commit murder two weeks before the homicide, and asked, if this were true, was she not the companion of the murderers and thieves, and that she was capable of the crime? He reminded the jury of Bridget's

proposal to ask Bush to write to Dr. Coriell, and her subsequent remarks about it in the same connection. According to her own statement, she gave no warning, though she knew who the murderers were. He cited also the conduct of the prisoner and accusing innocent persons; and inquired whether, in view of such conduct, she could be held to be wicked enough to murder Mrs. Coriell.

NYT 1 June 1867

After this address from Judge Vrendenburgh, it took only one hour for the jury to find Bridget Deignan (Durgan, Dergan) guilty of premeditated murder, and though the sentence was not pronounced that day, the people of New Market knew that Bridget would soon hang; the appeals process would do her no good. Bridget asked her lawyer, Mr. Adrian, if she could speak, insisting that she was not guilty and had not participated in any way in the murder of Mrs. Coriell. The judge told her attorney that she could not speak then, but she would be allowed to speak at her sentencing on June 17.

Before her sentencing, newspaper reporters from around the country, but especially from New York, New Jersey, and Pennsylvania, appeared in New Brunswick to interview Bridget, the prosecutors, the defense team, the jailers or anyone else involved in the Coriell murder trial. Some people, such as Mr. Brendan, had already visited a publishing house in Philadelphia with the first pages of the murder pamphlet about Bridget and her "life of crime" he planned to publish. A second murder pamphlet was in process as well, the second being titled *Life, Trial and Execution of Bridget Dergan*. Barclay & Co. publishers, also of Philadelphia, published it in 1867 just days after Bridget's hanging; there is no author credited. Because the process of printing these pamphlets took so much time in 1867, the printing of both pamphlets had to have begun before Bridget's execution, with the final pages being added after her death.

On June 17, 1867, Bridget was brought back before Judge Vrendenburgh to be sentenced. Her attorneys, Mr. Adrian and Mr. Leupp, began the proceeding by requesting a new trial based on the allowance of hearsay evidence and the prosecution's ascribing of a motive to Bridget that had not been corroborated by the witnesses. The judge denied the motion for a new trial. He then told Bridget that if she had anything to say to the court, she should say it then through her attorney. Before she quietly spoke to Mr. Adrian, she looked at every face in the courtroom gallery behind her; she appeared to be looking for someone whom she expected to speak up for her. She whispered something to Adrian, who then addressed the court. Mr. Adrian stated that, according to Bridget, there was a person "at large" who promised to tell the truth about Mrs. Coriell's murder and promised to testify to her innocence. She insisted she was not guilty and could not reveal more than she had because of an oath she'd taken on a Bible.

Judge Vrendenburgh responded by pronouncing sentence. He asserted the jury's certain belief that Bridget committed willful and premeditated murder in a manner that was cruel and horrible. He sentenced her to hang on August 30, 1867.

```
As soon as the fatal sentence was pronounced,
Bridget sat down, and rocking her body to and
fro, commenced to cry piteously, giving utter-
ance to screams that could be heard far beyond
the court house. She was removed to the jail,
where, for some time her lamentations were con-
tinued so loud that they could be heard by per-
sons without the enclosure.
```
NYT 18 June 1867

Six

There were circumstances surrounding this case that perhaps seemed to indicate that other persons beside the prisoner were engaged in the murder.

—George Robeson

As her execution grew closer, the fascination with the "murderess" in jail in New Brunswick swelled. Newspapers around the country continued to print reviews of the case with details and, in many instances, confessions. "The unfortunate woman has been solicited time and again to make a full confession of the crime, and her connection with it, and on three different occasions has done so, all of her confessions being more or less conflicting" (*Evening Telegraph* 29 August 1867). Evidence suggests that the reported confessions were just collections of answers to questions posed to Bridget by numerous people, including the jailers, prosecutors, and the district attorney. "These statements were made in reply to various questions, which she answered reluctantly, sometimes refusing to reply, and, at times, making no answer at all" (*NYT* 3 June 1867). Her statements were recorded and crafted by the press to organize and modify the multiple stories she'd told over time. The final telling by the press, however, included her guilt.

Sometime before her execution, Bridget decided that keeping her secret—the "removal of her encumbrance"—and compelling Mary Gilroy to also keep that secret, was the only goal she could achieve in her life and her only purpose. Mary's presence in the jail served as a reminder to Bridget that her secret was at risk. Once Bridget realized that there was no avoiding the gallows, she began to believe that clearing Mary Gilroy would keep her secret, allowing her to receive the last rites of her Catholic faith, and be buried in a Catholic cemetery.

Obviously, at some point before the actual murder, perhaps even before her abortion, Bridget must have confided in Mary about her father's stories and about his insistence that his daughter should follow the prophetic "ball of thread" if it unwound and directed her toward her new life. Mary's dropped ball of yarn from the jail cell above Bridget's had become the only magic clew for Bridget to follow—if not into a new life, at least out of the old. In fact, just before her execution, she took responsibility for the murder, but she did so only after resigning herself to her fate and deciding that clearing Mary Gilroy's name would keep her secret. No report suggests that Bridget offered a "confession" until it became clear to her that there would be no reprieve, and she would certainly die on the gallows. Bridget continued to insist to reporters and to her friends, Mary Randolph and Margaret Sullivan, that her heart and conscience were clear and that she had no guilt in the death of Mrs. Coriell; however, she also began to tell the jailers and the prosecutors that Mary Gilroy was not the guilty party.

Just before her execution, Mr. Herbert, the prosecutor in the Coriell murder case, visited Bridget and afterward told the press that Bridget had confessed to him. The confession that Herbert claims Bridget offered was essentially different from all the other descriptions she'd given of that night, but all her stories had been different enough that very few people really questioned Herbert's account. His final version of the night of the murder included Bridget's desire to marry the doctor, a circumstance no other person or witness had even suggested except Mr. Herbert himself at her trial. It seems Mr. Herbert was able to sell his version of Bridget's confession for publication to at least one newspaper.

It's interesting that Mr. Herbert, even after his attacks in court against Bridget's morality and even her humanity would present himself as the one person to whom Bridget would confide her true and honest confession. In fact, when the question of a possible commutation of Bridget's sentence from death by hanging to life in prison was presented to the governor, Herbert had written a specific and scathing letter to Governor Ward, insisting that it was against the interests of justice to do anything other than execute the convicted prisoner by hanging on August 30, 1867. Governor Ward had taken Herbert at his word and refused to commute Bridget's sentence. But again, Herbert insisted that he alone held the trust of the condemned person to tell her story.

This is very similar to the claim made by Brendan in his murder pamphlet. He stated that Bridget found only he was worthy of the truth of her story. "I will write it down now, and give it to Mr. Brendan; as he is the only one I think anything of at all. I am not friendly to these newspaper fellows; for they set everybody down against me. I will give this to Mr. Brendan before I leave this cell to go to the gallows down in the yard tomorrow" (Brendan 22).

Interestingly, aside from the fact that Bridget could neither read nor write is the fact that the Brendan murder pamphlet called Bridget a "wild beast" as well as "too ignorant and vicious" (42) to respond to the kindnesses of the good Christian people who wanted to save her soul. "The more desperate and wicked the criminal is and the more deplorably wicked is his or her offence, the greater number of those well disposed but unthinking people flock to the cell to offer consolation and direct the mind to heaven" (42). However, his pamphlet stressed that only he was loved and trusted enough by Bridget to tell her story for her.

LIFE, CRIMES, AND CONFESSION

OF

BRIDGET DURGAN,

THE FIENDISH MURDERESS OF MRS. CORIEL;

WHOM SHE BUTCHERED, HOPING TO TAKE HER PLACE
IN THE AFFECTIONS OF THE HUSBAND OF HER
INNOCENT AND LOVELY VICTIM.

THE ONLY AUTHENTIC, AND HITHERTO UNPUBLISHED

HISTORY OF HER WHOLE LIFE; AND THE HIDEOUS CRIME
FOR WHICH SHE WAS EXECUTED AT NEW BRUNSWICK, N. J.

BY REV. MR. BRENDAN.

PHILADELPHIA.
C. W. ALEXANDER, PUBLISHER.
224 South Third Street.

Entered according to Act of Congress, in the year 1867, by C. W. ALEXANDER, in the Clerk's Office of the District Court in and for the Eastern District of Pennsylvania.

Bridget's Hanging

Even more ironic is the fact that Brendan ended his murder pamphlet by recalling a "rumor" that Bridget was the one-time wife of convicted murderer Antoine Probst. Probst was an immigrant Catholic laborer in Pennsylvania who, in 1866, was convicted of the ax murders of an entire family, including four children ages eight years to fourteen months, as well as a cousin and another laborer who lived with the family.

> **BRIDGET DURGAN'S LIFE AND CRIMES**
>
> **BRIDGET DURGAN AND ANTOINE PROBST.**
>
> Among numbers of rumors that have been circulated about Bridget Durgan the miserable subject of the preceeding pages, was one to the effect that she was at one time the reputed wife of Antoine Probst, who it will be remembered, was the perpetrator of the atrocious Dearing murder.
>
> About the truth or falsity of this assertion, we have been unable to ascertain anything positively, and it would, therefore, be unfair, even to such a wretch as Bridget Durgan, to record such a thing against her as being true.
>
> Her name, and her grave are already sufficiently dishonored by her own wicked deeds, without adding more infamy to the load already on them. But one thing is certain, and that is, that, so far as inclination, temperament, and disposition were concerned, there never were two human beings more alike than Antoine Probst and Bridget Durgan. Both were possessed of the most depraved animal instincts, the most violent passion and the greatest blood thirstiness. A gentleman, accustomed all his life to criminals, said of Bridget:
>
> "She is the most perfect combination of the wolf, the tiger, the hog and the hyena, that I ever came across."
>
> The whole period during which Bridget was in prison, her constant anxiety was as to the amount of excitement she was producing. And so she continued till an hour or two before her execution; when she gave up all things and thoughts, except of death.
>
> Her history will doubtless make wives very cautious about what kind of women they have in their households as domestics.

From *Life, Crimes and Confession of Bridget Durgan*, http://publicdomainreview.org/collections/life-crimes-and-confession-of-bridget-durgan-1867/

Like Bridget, Antoine Probst was often misunderstood when he spoke because of his accent; he was also convicted by a jury in a matter of minutes. Probst's murder pamphlet, entitled *The Life, Confession and Atrocious Crimes of Antoine Probst, the Murderer of the Deeering Family; to which is added a Graphic Account of Many of the Most Horrible and Mysterious Murders Committed in this and Other Countries*, had been a best seller in multiple states. Barclay & Company of Philadelphia published the Antoine Probst Murder Pamphlet in 1866.

http://lawcollections.library.cornell.edu/bookreader/sat:1709/#page/1/mode/1up

Bridget's Hanging

This same company published a murder pamphlet in 1867 entitled, *Life, Trial and Execution of Bridget Dergan, who Murdered Mrs. Ellen Coriell, the Lovely Wife of Dr. Coriell, of New Market, N J, to which is added Her Full Confession and an Account of Her Execution at New Brunswick*. The murder pamphlet about Bridget published by Barclay & Co., did not assert or imply that she'd been the wife of Antoine Probst.

Taken altogether, many people made quite a bit of money telling Bridget's story in the press. In retrospect, it mattered little to the writers or to the readers whether the accounts were true. They were interesting and salacious, and they reinforced the anti-Catholic, anti-immigrant nationalistic culture that pervaded American consciousness at the time. In his book *"The Penalty Is Death": U.S. Newspaper Coverage of Women's Executions*, Marlin Shipman discusses the vilification of women accused of crimes in the media. He uses the term, "human garbage" to describe the adjectives used by the media when referencing individuals who will be executed:

> A few days before New Jersey executed Bridget Durgan, newspapers in that state and in nearby New York City ran an article describing her as "on the very lowest level" of human intelligence. She concealed her real actions, as did "the fox, the panther, and many inferior animals, whose instincts are more clearly defined than those of Bridget Durgan." Her head revealed "her strong animal organization," because "she is large in the base of the brain, and swells out over the ears, where distinctiveness and secretiveness are located by phrenologists, while the whole region of her intellect, ideality and moral sentiment is small." Durgan's eyes winked and wavered constantly, and they "open across, not below, the ball, and the pupil is uncommonly small... It is purely the eye of a reptile in shape and expression."
>
> (Shipman 171)

Mrs. Elizabeth Oakes Smith, a woman from a wealthy publishing family, wrote the quotes that Shipman took from the actual newspaper article. In the 1830s, she'd become, through the assistance of her magazine-editor husband, a writer, lecturer, and, ironically, a women's rights activist... seemingly less interested in the rights of noncitizen women and slaves (her son was arrested for transporting slaves in the 1850s and was providing munitions assistance to the Confederate cause).

Oakes Smith described herself as a suffragette, a warrior for the rights of women, and a visitor to women in prison so that she could better understand women in general. She would often visit women in "poverty, misery and even in prisons," then she would describe her new understanding of them in prose that she sold for publication or used in her lectures. With respect to the conviction of Bridget Deignan, she described Bridget's impending hanging as an example for all servants so that their mistresses could hire domestic workers without fear: "In this case I observe the women are unanimous in the feeling (for it is hardly an opinion) that she ought to be hung. Many believe that housekeepers will not be safe unless an example is made in this most atrocious case" (*NYT* 25 August 1867). She further described Bridget saying, "There is not one character of beauty, even in the lowest degree, about the girl; not one ray of sentiment, nothing genuine, hardly human, except a weak, sometimes a bitter, smile. The wonder is that any housekeeper should be willing to engage such a servant. I have an idea that this same girl was offered to me in an intelligence office in Brooklyn, and I refused to even talk with one so repulsive in appearance" (8/25/67).

Shipman's assertion that Bridget's humanity had been lost in the reporting of her own story, that she'd become human garbage, easily discarded could not be truer. Significant also is that Mary Ellen Coriell's humanity had been lost in the thousand bottles of ink spilled on this principally fiction story.

Numerous other people were selling their own versions of Bridget Deignan's (Durgan's or Dergan's) life story and making some money

Bridget's Hanging

doing so. But each printed story, each murder pamphlet, and each retelling (even this one) is different from every other story. On August 28, 1867, the *New York Times* printed the following:

> The sheriff is beset with applicants for tickets of admission to the jail-yard to witness the final scene in the life of the miserable woman. Between 400 and 500 tickets had been issued. The jail is daily visited by a great many persons, most of them ladies, anxious to see Bridget. The turnkey informs me that today he turned away as many as 200 persons from the jail door. I visited Bridget to-day. She seemed in excellent spirits, or anxious to appear so. She laughed nervously very frequently during the interview, and convulsively clasped the bars of the grated door. She said she was tired of being there and was glad she was so near her death. She spoke without agitation of her approaching execution, and said she was not afraid to die. On her bed lay several books, among them the Bible and prayer-books. She said laughingly that her Bible (meaning the Catholic Bible) was a better book than the protestant Bible, and seemed anxious to provoke a discussion on the subject.
>
> She has expressed the desire to the jail-keeper that no post-mortem examination be made in her case. The body of Williams the last person hanged in that jail yard was dissected in the jail-yard immediately after it was cut down from the gallows, and it was because she was aware of this fact that she made the request.

Bridget's fear of being stripped bare and dissected in the jail yard became an addendum to this misfortune of murder and execution. The postscript to the story seems less about her dignity and more about the end of the tale: it would end when the jailers cut her down, not when they opened her flesh on a wooden table in an open-air autopsy.

Bridget, it seems, was very much concerned about what a dissection of her body would prove regarding her abortion and the effect such knowledge would have on her burial in a Catholic Cemetery. She had been receiving counsel from two Catholic priests who had, it seems, granted her "extreme unction," or the last rites of the Catholic Church. According to that Church, the sacramental grace of Catholic confession is granted by God after the ritual blessing of holy oil. However, in Bridget's mind, burial in a Catholic cemetery would guarantee her an unfettered entrance into heaven, and she would finally achieve her landing on the Isle of the Blest.

```
The court of pardons having unanimously con-
firmed the sentence of the court, and Gov. Ward
having but two days ago declared in a letter to
the prosecuting attorney, that this section of
the court of pardons was intended to be final
in the case, all the preparations for her ex-
ecution are completed and by midday tomorrow,
Brigid Durkin will be a lifeless lump of clay.
The gallows on which the Negro Joseph Williams
was executed, on 5 July, still stands in the
jail yard ready for its victim. An intense de-
sire to witness the shocking tragedy seems to
possess almost everyone in this locality, and
Sheriff Clarkson has been sorely persecuted by
applicants for admission to the prison on the
```

> morning of the execution. Over 400 tickets have been issued, so that the affair promises to be anything but private. Immediately after the body of Joseph Williams was cut down, it underwent a dissection at the hands of the attending physicians. Bridget is aware of this fact, and she has earnestly requested the prison keeper that he will not permit a postmortem examination in her case. It is to be hoped that this request will be complied with, and that the remains of the unfortunate woman will be consigned to their last resting place without undergoing mutilation.
>
> Evening Telegraph 29 August 1867

Bridget's confused beliefs, according to the Protestant ideals of Mary Randolph and Margaret Sullivan, were bizarre and confounding. They both believed that anything that had occurred in New Market or anywhere else was fully known by God, and the disposition of a person's body had nothing to do with forgiveness or entrance into a spiritual union with God. But both also knew that Bridget was a simple and inexplicable young woman who held tightly to a combination belief of old Irish mythology and a long-dead Catholic understanding of tricking God with purchased indulgences, statues with sacred power, magical oils, and blessings. What could they say, they asked each other, that might save her soul? The article in the *New York Times* (8/28/1867) demonstrated that Bridget had chosen her old-world Catholic belief over the beliefs of Mary Randolph and Margaret Sullivan. She'd insisted to a reporter that the Catholic Bible was a better book than the Protestant Bible, but Bridget had already proven she could understand neither. Either through the intervention of her priests or the influence of Mary Gilroy, also from superstitious rural Ireland, Bridget had chosen to leave this world with, to the best of her ability, her terrible secret buried with her in Catholic soil.

On 31 August 1867, the *New York Times* printed the following story:

> Of her ability to perpetrate the murder in the way she describes in her "confession" there must be every doubt in the minds of reasoning people. Her alleged motive, the desire to take Mrs. Coriell's place, the use of a kerosene lamp as her first murderous weapon, her declaration that after she had hacked the body of Mrs. Coriell till she believed her victim was dead, and that the poor lady afterward followed her to the garden; thence returning, at the bidding of the murderess, to be hacked over again, all these details show that the true story of the murder is not yet told.
>
> It is unfortunate that our civilization does not permit us to be relieved of such without the disgraceful accompaniments of a levee in the condemned cell, and passports to Paradise written and sealed on the scaffold. More abominable curiosity, more mawkish sentimentality, more religious affectation, has been expended on this blood thirsty animal than we remember in the case of almost any other modern criminal. The atrocious spectacle of the hanging was properly concluded, when the filthy jailor who had charge of Durgan rushed into her embrace. The final tableau was a satire upon the forms of justice, and an insult to the poor woman who lies cold in her grave.

Bridget's Hanging

Whether reporters, writers or regular citizens believed that Bridget was a murderer, an animal, or an ignorant immigrant from a pagan country, her story had taken on a life of its own. Her story became both fodder for the anti-immigrant cause and an indictment of the movement for women's self-determination. The story became a sensational murder mystery novel for individuals who could read and the means for a few ambitious fiction writers to make some extra income at the expense of both Bridget and the Coriell family. This life-and-death story became, like so many other life-and-death stories, theater and entertainment.

Bridget was hanged on what was commonly called an upright jerker. When a jerker gallows was used, the noose rope was strung over the gallows' crossbeam, and the untied end was attached to a heavy weight. Once the noose was tightened around the neck of the person who was to be hanged, a securing rope was cut, and the pull created by the descent of the heavy weight "jerked" the condemned, in this case, Bridget, into the air with a violent surge and with the crack of the weight hitting the ground.

> Bridget Durgan, the New-Jersey murderess, was jerked into eternity yesterday morning, in an unseemly manner, in the presence of the roughest, rudest, and most ungentlemanly crowd of men we ever saw. Probably the execution of no person, with the single exception of Mrs. Surratt, has attracted such general attention and interest as hers.
>
> The cap was drawn, the signal given, and the rope severed. Up she went with a jerk, and the knot twisted to the back of her neck as her huge body fell to the length of the noose with a heavy thud. The strain was tremendous and her half-pinioned arms flew up. Officious officials

```
seized her hands and pulled them down, hold-
ing them while the contortions of her muscu-
lar frame afforded amplest gratification to the
noisy 'gentlemen' in front.
    After hanging a while and turning slowly
about, Bridget died, her pulse and heart ceasing
together. In thirty minutes she was lowered into
the coffin and the cap was about to be removed
when the priest interposed to prevent it, it hav-
ing been Bridget's request that her face should
not be seen. The Sheriff, however, insisted and
disclosed her pale, bloodless features to the
people who gathered to look. Her neck was not
broken and she died of strangulation.
```
New York Times 31 August 1867

And that was the end of the twenty-two tragic years of one person's life.

But that was not the end of this story. Dr. William Coriell, husband of Mrs. Mary Ellen Coriell, the murdered woman whose life seemed to have been lost in the ink and gossip of newspapers and murder pamphlets, died on May 25, 1881. He never remarried. He apparently moved to Plainfield, New Jersey, with his only child where he continued to work as a doctor and surgeon. He was buried in a Baptist cemetery in Plainfield. Mary Coriell, sometimes called Mamey, was unmarried in 1890 when she applied for her father's military pension. There were no other available records regarding Dr. Coriell's life after the murder of his wife, but there is a story implied in the fact that for fourteen years, a young, widowed doctor lived as a single man raising his daughter alone. In 1890, Mamey would have been twenty-five years old, old enough to have married and become a mother herself if she'd been so inclined. Whether she did eventually marry is not known.

Further, it was not the end of Mary Gilroy's public life. Mary, who was believed by many to be either the actual murderer of Mrs. Coriell or at least a conspirator and actor in the crime, was released after a grand jury failed to indict her in September 1867. According to the *New York Tribune*, "New Brunswick.—Mary Ann Gilroy, the supposed accomplice of Bridget Durgan in the Coriell Murder has been released from jail, the grand jury finding no indictment against her" (23 September 1867). Unlike the salacious details about the case against Bridget, this story was a tiny one-line blurb on page 8 of a single newspaper next to an ad for rubber goods and one for seltzer. Apparently, the public and the press were tired of the case. The attorney general and prosecutors could see that Mary Gilroy would not get their names in the paper. Census records show that Mary Gilroy left the area after being released from jail.

There are records from that period for at least five Mary Gilroys in the New York, New Jersey, and Pennsylvania area. Two were married and do not fit the age range of Mary McGinn Karr Gilroy. One Mary Gilroy was a socialite from Pennsylvania whose name often appeared in the press as participating in fundraisers and attending parties with well-heeled members of Pennsylvania society. Another Mary Gilroy was a seamstress in New York City whose name appeared in the *New York Times* after she and several other seamstresses had been defrauded by their employer. A fifth Mary Gilroy, who evidence suggests was the same Mary Gilroy jailed with Bridget Deignan in New Brunswick, appeared in a short article published in the *Evening Telegraph* newspaper of Philadelphia: "THEFT OF MONEY.—Mary Gilroy was taken into custody yesterday by Policeman Brady, of the Seventh district, upon the charge of the larceny of a pocket-book containing $36 from a house at Front and Coates Streets. Defendant had a hearing before Alderman Cahill, and was held in $600 bail to answer" (22 September 1870). Because $600 was a tremendous amount of money in 1870, it's probable that Mary Gilroy remained in jail for some time.

In 1880, a Mary Gilroy who fit the age and description of Mary McGinn Karr Gilroy, illiterate, born in Ireland, widowed, and without family, appears on the Danville, Pennsylvania, census records as an "inmate" or patient at the State Hospital for the Insane.

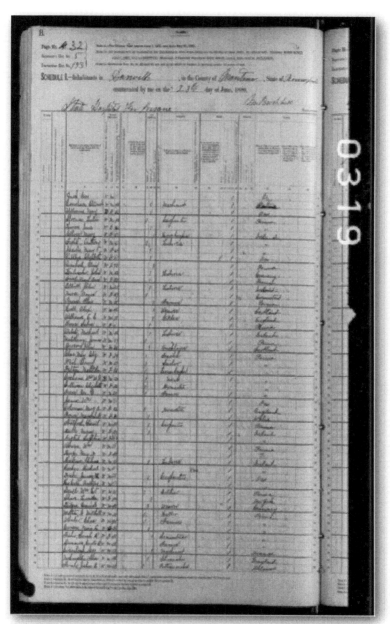

Federal Census: see line 6
https://familysearch.org
(Specific URLs subject to change)

Bridget's Hanging

The reason checked for her incarceration there is "insane." Prior to being committed, the records indicate, she worked as a housekeeper or housemaid. Mary Gilroy appears on the census documents for the Danville State Hospital for the Insane in 1900 and in 1910 as well. (Census records for 1890 are not available. "1890 census' population schedules were badly damaged by a fire in the Commerce Department Building in January 1921," according to the United States Census Bureau website.)

Sheila Duane

Federal Census: see line 28
https://familysearch.org

Bridget's Hanging

By 1910, it appears that Mary Gilroy could no longer communicate or could not communicate with any lucidity. Researchers have concluded that "x-ot" probably indicates "nonverbal" or "unavailable."

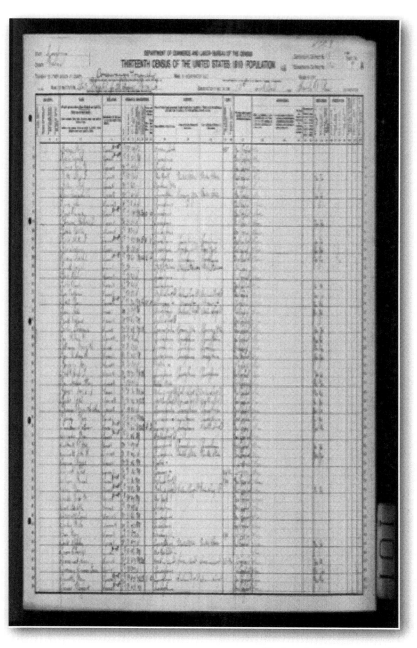

Federal Census: see line 39
https://familysearch.org

Bridget's Hanging

There are no available records of Mary Gilroy's death.

In her book *Women Who Kill*, Ann Jones compares the story of Bridget Deignan to that of Lizzie Borden. She states,

> In 1867, the household of Dr. William Coriell in New Market, New Jersey, employed a domestic by the name of Bridget Durgan. In 1892, the household of Mr. Andrew Borden in Fall River, Massachusetts, employed a domestic named Bridget Sullivan. (She, however, was known as Maggie, for Mr. Borden's daughter, Lizzie, found it so much simpler to call all the Irish servants who passed, one after another, through the household, by the same name.) The Coriell house and the Borden house came to have one other thing in common: each became the scene of an extraordinarily brutal and vicious murder. In both cases the killing took place within the house. No one saw it. In both cases the suspected murderer told confused and contradictory stories of what happened and tried to pin the crime on someone else. In both cases the suspect willfully destroyed physical evidence. In both cases, on the basis of highly incriminating circumstantial evidence, the suspected woman was charged with murder and brought to trial. And there all the resemblance stops.
>
> (228)

Jones goes on to discuss the differences between the press coverage of Lizzie's trial and Bridget's trial and the importance of Lizzie's status. The press described Lizzie using positive adjectives, saying she had "lustrous eyes," "dignity," and "a retiring manner." Reporters depicted her as being "of a sensitive nature," and one friend is quoted saying that Lizzie had committed "not one unmaidenly nor a single deliberately unkind act" (*Boston Herald* 6 August 1892). Her clothing was called high fashion and her eyes a lovely hue of brown. She was portrayed as feminine and ladylike, often fanning herself in the courtroom and appearing to be faint from the thought of the murders. Members of Lizzie's legal team were well known for their skill and knowledge of the law as well as their connections to Massachusetts upper-class society, "Miss Borden was represented by a panel of attorneys well-respected among the 'grey beards.' Andrew Jennings was a prominent citizen who for many years had been Andrew Borden's attorney. Melvin O. Adams, an experienced Boston trial lawyer, impressed the jury with his big city manners and waxed mustache. And George D. Robinson, at fifty-nine, a stately imposing gentleman of the old school, had served three times as governor of the Commonwealth" (Jones 248). And though Lizzie's father had been too miserly to provide for his family a wealthy lifestyle, Lizzie was still a respected white Protestant American woman who spoke English perfectly and was an established member of the Fall River, Massachusetts, community. The press and the jury found Lizzie not guilty.

Many people today still believe that Bridget Deignan murdered Mary Ellen Coriell. And certainly there is proof beyond a reasonable doubt that Bridget feared or knew about the impending robbery of the Coriell household when she walked into the barn and asked Asa Bush to write a note to Dr. Coriell, requesting he return home. But what factors mitigated her guilt? Can someone with a child's understanding foresee the possible consequences of her actions? And even if people choose to believe that she was guilty of conspiracy after the fact, if her reason for maintaining her silence was somehow linked to blackmail and her misunderstanding of her own salvation, shouldn't she have been granted life in a jail cell or in a hospital for the feebleminded?

Or is Bridget's narrative just another version of the same story that happens every day in this and every other country in the world? People who are wealthy, socially connected, or well established in their communities are given opportunities in the judicial system and in the press to secure verdicts of not guilty. People without wealth or standing or who don't fit intellectually or religiously or racially, immigrants, the undereducated, the othered, people with politically different ideas—these people are not allowed the opportunities that the emblematic citizens, the conventional, normal, conforming, middle-class and certainly upper-middle-class members of culture are granted by their status alone.

Maybe Bridget's story is just another in a long list of stories like it.

Sheila Duane

Image by Dean Duane

Bibliography

Andrews, William Loring. *The Iconography of the Battery and Castle Garden.* New York: Scribner, 1901. Print.

Billington, Ray. *The Protestant Crusade, 1800–1860.* New York: Macmillian, 1938. Print.

Brendan, Rev. Mr. *Life, Crimes and Confession of Bridget Durgan, the Fiendish Murderess of Mrs. Coriell; whom she Butchered Hoping to Take the Place in the Affections of the Husband of her Innocent and Lovely Victim. The Only Authentic, and Hitherto Unpublished History of her Whole Life; and the Hideous Crime for which She was Executed at New Brunswick, N.J.* Philadelphia: C.W. Alexander, 1867. Available at The Public Domain Review: http://publicdomainreview.org/collections/life-crimes-and-confession-of-bridget-durgan-1867/

Coogan, Tim P. *The Famine Plot: England's Role in Ireland's Greatest Tragedy.* New York: Macmillan, 2012. Print.

Cunningham, John T. *Murder Did Pay, 19th-Century New Jersey Murders.* Orange: New Jersey Historical Society, 1981. Print.

Dude, Annie. "Immigrant health." *Celebrating Women in American History.* New York: Facts On File, 2011. *American Women's History Online*, Facts On File, Inc. http://www.fofweb.com/activelink2.asp?ItemID=WE42&iPin=CWAHIIsb007&SingleRecord=True (accessed October 24, 2013).

Ernst, Robert. *Immigrant Life in New York City, 1825–1863.* 1949. Reprint, New York: Octagon Books, 1979. Print.

Foner, Nancy. *From Ellis Island to JFK: New York's Two Great Waves of Immigration.* New Haven, Conn.: Yale University Press, 2002. Print.

Hickey, Raymond. *Irish English: History and Present-Day Forms.* Cambridge: Cambridge University Press, 2007. Print.

Higham, John. *Strangers in the Land: Patterns of American Nativism, 1860–1925.* New York: Athenaeum, 1963. Print.

Jackson, Kenneth T., ed. *Encyclopedia of New York City.* New York: New York Historical Society, 1995. Print.

Jones, Ann. *Women Who Kill.* The Feminist Press at the City University of New York, 2009. Print.

Leonard, Ira and Robert D. Parmet, eds. *American Nativism, 1830–1860.* New York: Van Nostrand Reinhold, 1971. Print.

Life and Confession of Bridget Dergan who Murdered Mrs. Ellen Coriell, the Lovely Wife of Dr. Coriell, of New Market, NJ to which is added her Full Confession and an Account of her Execution at New Brunswick. Murder Pamphlet. Philadelphia: Barclay & Co., 1867. Reprinted in *Murder Did Pay* (see Cunningham).

MacLellan, Anne and Alice Mauger, eds. *Growing Pains: Childhood Illness in Ireland, 1750–1950.* Dublin: Irish Academic Press, 2013. Print.

Mawajdeh, Hady. "The case Against Bite Mark Evidence." *Texas Standard*, 2014. http://www.texasstandard.org/stories/why-bite-mark-evidence-shouldnt-be-used-in-courts/

McCarthy, John P. "Nineteenth-Century Ireland." *Ireland: A Reference Guide from the Renaissance to the Present*, European Nations. New York: Facts On File, Inc., 2006. *Modern World History Online*. Facts On File, Inc. http://www.fofweb.com/activelink2.asp?ItemID=WE53&iPin=IRL0005&SingleRecord=True (accessed October 24, 2013).

Moran, Gerard. Sending Out Ireland's Poor: Assisted Emigration to North America in the Nineteenth Century. Dublin: Four Courts Press, 2004. Print.

Montez, Lola. *The Arts of Beauty; Or, Secrets of a Lady's Toilet.* New York: Dick & Fitzgerald, 1858. Available through Harvard University Archives: https://archive.org/stream/artsbeautyorsec00montgoog#page/n14/mode/2up

Novatny, Ann. *Strangers at the Door: Ellis Island, Castle Garden, and the Great Migration to America.* Riverside: Chatham Press, 1972. Print.

Powell, John. "Castle Garden." *Encyclopedia of North American Immigration.* Facts On File, Inc., 2005. *American History Online*. Facts On File, Inc. http://www.fofweb.com/ activelink2.asp? ItemID=WE52&iPin=ENAI0054&SingleRecord=True (accessed October 24, 2013).

Shipman, Marlin. *The Penalty Is Death: U.S. Newspaper Coverage of Women's Executions.* Columbia, University of Missouri Press, 2002. Print.

Svejda, George J. *Castle Garden as an Immigrant Depot.* Washington, DC: Division of History, Office of Archaeology and Historic Preservation, 1968. Print.

Woodham-Smith, Cecil. *The Great Hunger: Ireland: 1845–1849*. London: Penguin, 1992.

CENSUS:

Census Documents: https://familysearch.org (Specific URLs subject to change).
Special thanks to the Church of Jesus Christ of Latter-day Saints.

The US National Archives and Records Administration.
https://www.archives.gov/

NEWSPAPERS:

Boston Journal, Boston, MA. 1833–1917.
http://chroniclingamerica.loc.gov/ (Specific URLs subject to change)

Boston Traveler, Boston, MA. 1845–1967.
http://chroniclingamerica.loc.gov/

Burlington Weekly Free Press, Burlington, VT. 1866–1928.
http://chroniclingamerica.loc.gov/

Clearfield Republican, Clearfield, PA. 1851–1937.
http://chroniclingamerica.loc.gov/

Daily National Intelligencer, Washington, DC. 1813–1869.
http://chroniclingamerica.loc.gov/

Evening Star, Washington, DC. 1854–1972.
http://chroniclingamerica.loc.gov/

The Jeffersonian, Stroudsburg, PA. 1853–1911.
   http://chroniclingamerica.loc.gov/

New Brunswick Daily Fredonian, New Brunswick, NJ. 1859–1886.
   Monmouth County Historical Association.

New York Tribune, New York, NY. 1866–1824.
   http://chroniclingamerica.loc.gov/

Richmond Dispatch, Richmond, VA. 1850–1884.
   http://chroniclingamerica.loc.gov/

Trenton State Gazette, Trenton NJ. 1863–1918.
   http://chroniclingamerica.loc.gov/

All *New York Times* articles from
   New York Times Article Archive
   http://www.nytimes.com/ref/membercenter/nytarchive.html

Special thanks to Ann Jones, author of *Women Who Kill*, *Kabul in Winter*, *Looking for Lovedu*, *When Love Goes Wrong*, *They Were Soldiers*, *War Is Not Over When It Is Over*, and *Next Time She'll be Dead*, for her scholarship and the strength of her voice.

Made in the USA
Middletown, DE
11 December 2016